KING LEAR

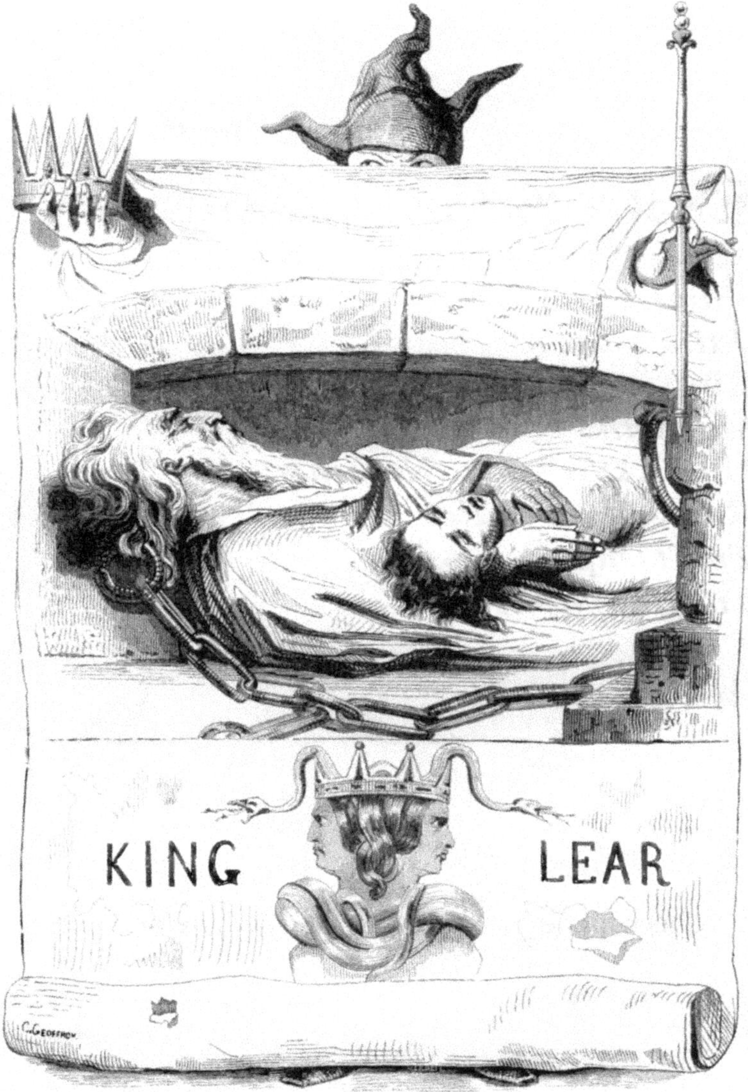

ENJOY SHAKESPEARE

Hamlet
Julius Caesar
King Lear
Macbeth
Much Ado About Nothing
Romeo and Juliet
The Tempest
Twelfth Night

Check for new titles at www.FullMeasurePress.com

ENJOY SHAKESPEARE

King Lear

By

William Shakespeare

A Verse Translation

By

Kent Richmond

2nd edition, revised

 Full Measure Press • Lakewood, California

Published by:
Full Measure Press
P.O. Box 6294
Lakewood, CA 90714-6294 USA

www.FullMeasurePress.com

© Copyright 2004, 2013 by Kent Richmond

All rights reserved. No part of this publication may be performed, reproduced, stored in a retrieval system, or transmitted in any form or by any means electronic, mechanical, photocopying, recording or otherwise, without the prior written permission of the author.

ISBN-13: 978-0-9836379-4-3

Printed in the United States of America

Contents

About this Translation 7
Notes on the Meter 8
About the Play 9
Characters in the Play 11
Which Text Was Used? 12

ACT ONE 13
Scene One. A Room of State in Lear's Palace 15
Scene Two. A Hall in Gloucester's Castle 28
Scene Three. A Room in Albany's Palace 35
Scene Four. A Hall in Albany's Palace 37
Scene Five. The Court before Albany's Palace 52

ACT TWO 55
Scene One. Court Within Gloucester's Castle 57
Scene Two. Outside Gloucester's Castle 63
Scene Three. The Open Country 71
Scene Four. Outside Gloucester's Castle 71

ACT THREE 85
Scene One. A Heath 87
Scene Two. Another Part of the Heath 89
Scene Three. A Room in Gloucester's Castle 93
Scene Four. A Part of the Heath with a Shed 94
Scene Five. A Room in Gloucester's Castle 102
Scene Six. In a Farmhouse Near the Castle 103
Scene Seven. A Room in Gloucester's Castle 108

ACT FOUR 115
Scene One. The Heath 117
Scene Two. Outside the Duke of Albany's Palace 121
Scene Three. The French Camp near Dover 126
Scene Four. A Tent in the French Camp 128
Scene Five. A Room in Gloucester's Castle 130
Scene Six. The Country Near Dover 132
Scene Seven. A Tent in the French Camp 145

6 • King Lear

ACT FIVE **151**
    Scene One. The British Camp near Dover 153
    Scene Two. A Field Between the Two Camps 157
    Scene Three. The British Camp near Dover 158
Endnotes 176
Sources 180
Facts about *King Lear* 181

Illustrations

Front Matter and page 182 illustrations are adapted from engravings by Ch. Geoffroy from *Galerie des Personnages de Shakespeare* (1844), compiled by Amédée Pichot (1795-1877). Paris: Baudry, Librairie Européenne.

Page 85 (Edgar sees the Fiend) and page 141 ("I am the king himself") by Sir John Gilbert (1817-1897) from the *Gilbert Shakespeare* (1857), edited by Howard Staunton. London and New York: George Routledge & Sons.

Page 91, from "The King and Fool in the Storm" by Charles Buchel (1872–1950) from *Cassell's Illustrated Shakespeare* (1913), New York and London: Funk and Wagnalls Co.

Page 121, "Mr. Fleming as Edgar" by E.A Chapman and S. Hallyer from the *Complete Works of Shakespeare* (1878) edited by Halliwell, Knight, Collier, and others.

Page 151, "Lear and Cordelia" by V.W. Bromley (1848-1877) from *The Royal Shakespeare* (1894), London, Paris, and Melbourne: Cassell and Company Limited.

Other illustrations from *Shakespeare in Pictorial Art* (1916) by Malcolm C. Salaman (text) and Charles Holme (ed.). London: "The Studio" Ltd. Page 13 and page 115, detail from paintings by Ford Maddox Brown (1821-1893); page 55, "Lear's Fool" by Frank Gillett (1874-1927); page 175, detail from "King Lear" by James Barry, R.A. (1741-1806), engraved by Francis Legat (1755-1809).

About this Translation

This translation makes the language of William Shakespeare's drama more contemporary without modernizing the play in any other way. No lines are omitted or simplified, and no characters or scenes are deleted.

My aim is for readers to experience Shakespeare's plays with the level of challenge and comprehension offered to audiences 400 years ago. Despite the richness of the plays, theatergoers in that era did not need scene summaries to follow the plot, footnotes to interpret vocabulary, or elaborate gestures to help them recognize a joke or guess at the character's intentions or emotional state. After all, Shakespeare's characters tell us what they are thinking. The plays lasted only a couple of hours, which means the actors spoke at a fairly rapid, though comfortable, pace.

To qualify this translation as authentic Shakespeare, I preserve the metrical rhythm of the original as much as possible. When the original employs iambic pentameter, this translation does too. When characters speak in prose, the translation shifts to prose. Rhymes, the occasional alliteration, and metrical irregularities are preserved. Jokes, inspired or lame, and poetic devices get equivalents in the modern language. Sentence length and syntactic complexity are the same.

To help comprehension, I occasionally add brief pieces of exposition, careful to operate within the metrical constraints imposed by the original. Shakespeare sometimes makes references to Greek mythology and folk legends, many of which are obscure today. So Hecate becomes "the sorcery of Hecate," or Phoebus becomes "the Sun God." This practice eliminates the need for footnotes, which are unavailable to the theater audience and a distraction to readers. The occasional endnote offers an alternate translation of a disputed passage or explains a decision to deviate from the original. Endnotes can be ignored without loss of comprehension.

I suggest reading this translation without referring to the original so that you can imagine the play as theater in real time with the rhythm and pacing undisturbed. Don't be surprised if the "colors" seem a bit brighter than you remember them. After four centuries, more than a little "linguistic grime" builds up as our language changes. Keep in mind how surprised we are when Renaissance paintings are restored to their original state and those muted, sepia hues turn into celebrations of color. My translation wants you to see the same colors that the groundlings and the royalty saw when they crowded into theaters 400 years ago.

Kent Richmond

Notes on the Meter

Shakespeare's plays mix blank verse (unrhymed iambic pentameter), prose, and songs. They also include couplets or other rhyme schemes to close scenes and heighten dramatic exchanges. This translation preserves these forms, assuming Shakespeare had a dramatic justification for these swings between blank verse, prose, and rhyme.

In translating songs, I mimic the rhythm and find suitable rhymes, but Shakespeare's iambic pentameter is more problematic and requires decisions as to what constitutes a metrical line. His plays, especially the later ones, are full of short lines, long lines, lines with extra syllables, and other deviations from the expected ten-syllable line. If a line seems deviant, was Shakespeare sloppy? Is the text corrupt? Has the pronunciation changed? Or was he aiming for some dramatic effect?

Shakespeare did not leave us polished editions of his plays. But several hundred years of tinkering by scholars has provided the polishing and copy editing that Shakespeare failed to do. I have taken advantage of that scholarship and assume that any remaining anomalies are part of Shakespeare's design and must be respected. If the deviant meter is due to pronunciation change, then I find a metrical equivalent in contemporary English. If not, then the translation deviates in the same way as the original.

Of course no translation can perfectly capture both the sense and sound of poetry. When conflicts arise, I favor sense over strict adherence to the rhythm. Yet I do not allow a line to have a rhythm not found in Shakespeare's verse at the time he wrote the play.

For more information on Shakespeare's verse, see my article "How Iambic Pentameter Works" (available at www.FullMeasurePress.com/Iambic_Pentameter.html).

About the Play

In *King Lear*, Shakespeare turns a mostly legendary story with a happy ending into one of the most brilliant, disturbing, and emotionally-taxing dramas ever staged. In the original story, an aging British king in the pre-Roman era divides his kingdom into equal parts to provide dowries for his three daughters. Two daughters, Regan and Goneril, after shamelessly flattering the king, receive their shares and marry dukes, but the third and favorite daughter, Cordelia, is banished when she refuses to exaggerate her love. Eventually Lear loses all his power to Regan and Goneril and is reduced to poverty. He reunites with Cordelia, now married to the King of the Franks, and the two raise an army that successfully recovers the kingdom.

Shakespeare keeps the basic plot but disposes of the happy ending. He adds an equally disturbing and brutal subplot in which Edmund, the Earl of Gloucester's illegitimate son, turns his gullible father against his half-brother Edgar. Shakespeare even tosses in that staple of comedy, the Fool, but this fool is an ill-fated, "bitter" one who shares Lear's suffering. The Folio edition of Shakespeare's works (1623) added the word *tragedy* to the title, and it seems a necessary warning. Prepare for a play that assaults the senses and tests endurance.

This relentlessness shows in the first scene, where all but two major characters appear. Lear calmly delivers what seems a well-thought-out plan but quickly becomes enraged and banishes both Cordelia and Kent, a loyal follower who protests. This turn of events allows Regan and Goneril, who privately acknowledge Lear's foolishness without openly protesting it, to extend their power and marginalize Lear. By the end of Act 2, after shocking confrontations with his daughters, Lear is stripped of his remaining privileges, and Edgar is a fugitive.

When Act 3 ends, villains hold nearly all the power, leaving the rest homeless, even eyeless, in a land torn by civil war and invasion. By the play's end, only three major characters survive to piece together Lear's kingdom.

Just as relentless is the language. The opening speeches of Lear, Regan, and Goneril are smooth and ceremonial, but the characters soon break from that form as the kingdom falls apart and true colors show. Lear's descent into rage and madness stretches the limits of blank verse and the endurance of the actor who plays him. Lear's Fool and Edgar's Poor Tom pound us with a mixture of sense and nonsense, while Regan and Goneril change from glib, patronizing manipulators into vindictive, frenzied thugs. There are tender moments when Lear comforts his fool, Edgar describes Dover, and Lear reunites with Cordelia, but the rest is a masterpiece of brutal, intense poetic expression.

The language also points to philosophical and moral themes running through the play. The words *kind/kindly/kindness* appear over 20 times, *natural/unnatural/nature* over 40 times, *need/necessity* nearly 30 times, and *nothing* about 35 times. Lear, despite his anger and rashness, is described as a kind king by his loyal followers. But kindness toward his daughters contributes to his destruction as his own offspring rebel against the natural ties that bind parent and child. Edmund, the "natural" son of Gloucester, invokes nature as his goddess in a cynical justification for his villainy. But he too is doomed, so neither kindness nor unrestrained villainy alone can weather this storm. The talk of need begins at the end of Act 2 when Regan and Goneril remove the last of Lear's knights and the formerly pampered Lear explores what it means to need and to have nothing.

Too many good people, or at least redeemable ones, die in *King Lear* to leave us comfortable with the ending. But the play does not seem to surrender to despair, chaos, and amorality. The survivors, after all, are good people, and the villains are gone. Perhaps we should see it as a twisted fairy tale for adults. Like a fairy tale, it takes place in a far-off time, offers few details on the characters' history or culture, and does not overtly moralize. Yet after hearing it we have a better sense of how power works, how the good behave, and what we must guard against.

So imagine the play beginning, "Once upon a time, there was a kind, old king with three daughters who...."

Characters in the Play

Lear Household (at the start of the play)
  LEAR, King of Britain
  GONERIL, eldest daughter of Lear
  REGAN, daughter of Lear
  CORDELIA, youngest daughter of Lear
  Lear's **FOOL**
  KNIGHTS attending on the King

Gloucester Household
  Earl of **GLOUCESTER**
  EDGAR, son of Gloucester (later disguised as Poor Tom)
  EDMUND, illegitimate son of Gloucester
  OLD MAN, tenant of Gloucester
  CURAN, a gentleman

King of **FRANCE**, suitor and eventual husband to Cordelia
Duke of **BURGUNDY**, suitor to Cordelia
Duke of **CORNWALL**, husband of Regan
Duke of **ALBANY**, husband of Goneril
Earl of **KENT**, follower of Lear (later disguised as Caius)

OSWALD, steward to Goneril
PHYSICIAN, serving Cordelia and Lear
GENTLEMAN, serving Cordelia
5 other **GENTLEMEN**
a **HERALD**
3 **SERVANTS** to Cornwall
3 **OFFICERS**
a **CAPTAIN**, a follower of Edmund

2 **MESSENGERS**

Officers, Soldiers, and Attendants

                    Scene: Britain

Which Text Was Used?

This revised edition of *King Lear: A Verse Translation*, in addition to substantial changes in the translation itself, shows more clearly the textual origins of the play.

Shakespeare's *King Lear* survives in more than one version. The First Quarto (1608) and the similar Second Quarto (1619) have about 300 lines not in the Folio (1623). The better edited Folio has about 100 lines not in the Quarto plus hundreds of other differences.

To provide as complete a translation of *King Lear* as possible, this translation tends toward the version found in the Folio but includes material from the Quarto deleted in the Folio.

Material added from the Quarto is found between single angled quotation marks ‹ ›. Material in the Folio not in the Quarto is marked with double-angled quotation marks « ». Differences shorter than one line are not marked.

Line Numbers

Prose lines count as a new line whenever they break. Shared verse lines count as one line. Verse lines too long to fit on one line receive a hanging indent and count as one line.

King Lear

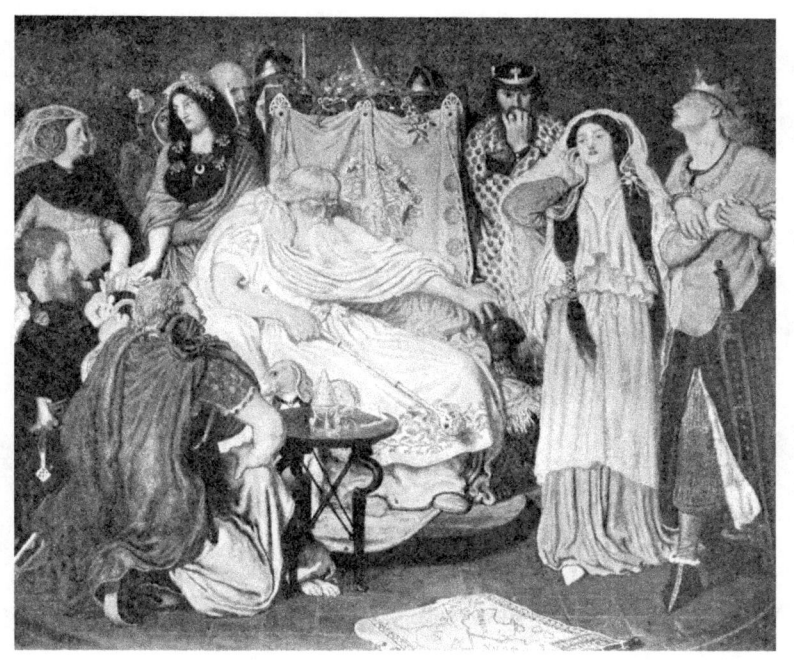

Act One

Act One

Scene One. A Room of State in Lear's Palace

[Enter KENT, GLOUCESTER, and EDMUND]

KENT (Earl of Kent, follower of Lear)
I thought the King favored the Duke of Albany more than Cornwall.

GLOUCESTER (Earl of Gloucester)
It always seemed so to us, but now with this division of the kingdom, it's not clear which duke he values most, for their portions are so carefully weighed that the closest scrutiny reveals no advantage in either share.

KENT
Isn't this your son, my lord?

GLOUCESTER
His parentage, sir, has been at my expense. I've blushed so often in acknowledging him that I'm immune to it.

KENT
I had no conception.

GLOUCESTER
Sir, this young fellow's mother surely did, at which point her womb grew round, and had indeed, sir, a son for her cradle before she had a husband for her bed. Do you detect a sin?

KENT
I do not wish a sin undone when its outcome seems so fit.

GLOUCESTER
I also have a legitimate son, sir, a year or so older than this one, whose value in my account is no higher. This young chap came somewhat impertinently into the world before he was sent for, yet his mother was a beauty, there was good sport in making him, and so the dear bastard must be acknowledged. Do you know this noble gentleman, Edmund?

EDMUND (illegitimate son of Gloucester)
No, my lord.

GLOUCESTER
My Lord of Kent. Remember him hereafter as my honored friend.

EDMUND
I offer my respect to your lordship.

KENT
I owe you my friendship and beg to know you better.

EDMUND
Sir, I'll make myself deserving of it.

GLOUCESTER
He has been away for nine years, and away he shall go again. [sound of a trumpet] The king is coming.

   [Enter LEAR, CORNWALL, ALBANY, GONERIL, REGAN, CORDELIA, and ATTENDANTS]

LEAR (King of Britain)
Bring in the lords of France and Burgundy, Gloucester.

GLOUCESTER
I shall, my liege.

   [Exit GLOUCESTER and EDMUND]

LEAR
Meanwhile the murkier details of my plan.
Give me the map there. Note that I've divided
My kingdom into thirds: my firm intent's 35
To shed all cares and duties in old age
And pass them on to younger powers, «while I,
Unburdened, crawl toward death. My sons-in-law,
You, Cornwall, and my no less loving Albany,
I am determined to proclaim this hour 40
Each daughters' dowry so that future strife
May now be sorted out.»*
The two great princes, France and Burgundy,
Fine rivals for my youngest daughter's love,
Have in this court paid long and amorous visits, 45
And now are to be answered. Tell me, my daughters—
«Since now I will divest myself of rule,
Title to territory, cares of state—»
Which of you three should I say loves me most
So I can then extend my largest bounty 50
To where the claim's both natural and merited?
Goneril, my eldest-born, speak first.

GONERIL (eldest daughter of Lear)
Sir, my love for you is more than words can wield,
Dearer than eyesight, space to live, and freedom,
Beyond what is appraised as rich or rare, 55
No less than life, with grace, health, beauty, honor;
As much as child can give or father find;
A love that makes voice poor and speech inept:
Beyond all measure and compare I love you.

CORDELIA (youngest daughter of Lear)
[aside] What should Cordelia say? Love, and be silent. 60

LEAR
All of these regions, from this line to that,
With shady forests and with fertile plains,
With plenteous rivers and extensive fields,
I leave to you—to yours and Albany's offspring

---

* Page 14 explains the function of these angled quotation marks.

In perpetuity. My second daughter, 65
My dearest Regan, wife to Cornwall, speak.

REGAN (daughter of Lear)
I'm made of that same fabric as my sister,
So price me at her worth. In my true heart
I too have filed this deed of love she's drawn;
Only she falls too short in that I see 70
Myself an enemy even to those joys
That carefully balanced sensibilities
Allow[1] and find my happiness derives
Alone from love for you.

CORDELIA
[aside]   Next poor Cordelia!
Perhaps not so since I am sure my love 75
Outweighs my tongue.

LEAR
For you and for your progeny forever
Remains this ample third of my fair kingdom,
No less in space, in value, and in pleasures
Than that bequeathed to Goneril. Now, my joy, 80
Though last but not the least, to whose young love
«The vines of France and milk of Burgundy
Strive to be linked,» what can you say to gain
A third more opulent than your sisters? Speak.

«CORDELIA
Nothing, my lord. 85

LEAR
Nothing?»

CORDELIA
Nothing.

LEAR
Nothing can come of nothing. Speak again.[2]

CORDELIA
Unhappy though it makes me, I cannot heave
My heart into my mouth. I love as much 90
As duty can demand—no more, no less.

LEAR
Come now, Cordelia? Add more to your speech,
Or your endowment is at risk.

CORDELIA
                              My lord,
You've fathered, raised, and loved me. In return,
I've been as dutiful as is expected, 95
Obeyed you, loved you, and so honored you.
Why have my sisters wed if all their love
Is owed to you? It's likely, when I wed,
The lord whose hand receives my vows will carry
Half my love with him, half my care and duty. 100
I'm sure I'll never marry like my sisters,
⟨Only to love my father.⟩

LEAR
Your heart agrees with this?

CORDELIA
                    It does, my lord.
LEAR
So young and so untender?

CORDELIA
So young, my lord, and true. 105

LEAR
Let it be so. Your truth will be your dowry!
For by the sacred radiance of the sun,
The sorcery of Hecate, and the night,
By all the power of the stars above,
Which govern when we live or cease to be, 110
I disavow paternal obligations,
Relation and all claims on me through blood,

And as a stranger to my heart and me,
Deny you these forever. Barbarous Scythians, 115
Or those who feast upon their progeny
To gorge their appetites, will be as welcome
Here to my bosom, pitied and assisted,
As you my one-time daughter.

KENT
       My good king—

LEAR
Peace, Kent.
Don't come between the dragon and his wrath. 120
I loved her most and planned to wager all
On her kind care! [to Cordelia] Away and leave my
 sight!—
My only peace is death, as I remove
Her father's heart from her! Call France.

  [shocked ATTENDANTS do not respond]

          Obey!
Call Burgundy.—Cornwall and Albany, 125

   [ATTENDANT exits]

My other daughters will divide her third.
Let pride, which she calls frankness, be her dowry.
I will endow you jointly with my power,
With sole authority, and all the trappings
That come with majesty. And month by month 130
Retaining for my use one hundred knights,
Provided me by you, I'll alternate
Residing with you two. I'll still retain
My title and all honors due a king.
But revenue, control, all other charges— 135
Belovèd sons, they're yours; to make this firm,
This crown is split between you.

 [Keeps his crown but gives a smaller crown, previously
  intended for Cordelia, to Albany and Cornwall]

KENT
                    Royal Lear,
Whom I have always honored as my king,
Loved as my father, followed as my master,
As my great patron thought of in my prayers...   140

LEAR
The bow is bent and drawn. Avoid the shaft.

KENT
Let it strike even if its barbs invade
The tissues of my heart. Kent must be blunt
When Lear is mad. What would you do, old man?³
Do you think duty will not dare to speak   145
If power bows to flattery? Honor calls for frankness
When majesty falls to folly. Retain your kingdom,
And use your soundest judgment to curtail
This hideous rashness. Slay me if I err:
Your youngest daughter does not love you least   150
And can't be empty-hearted if her voice
Does not sound hollow.

LEAR
                    Kent, on your life, no more.

KENT
My life I've always seen as but a stake
To bet against your enemies, not fear its loss,
Your safety my incentive.

LEAR
                    Out of my sight!   155

KENT
See better, Lear, and let me always be
The target in the center of your eye.

LEAR
Now, by Apollo—

KENT
                    Now by Apollo, king,
You call your gods in vain.

LEAR
                         O slave! O infidel! [laying his
    hand on his sword]

**«ALBANY (husband of Goneril) and CORNWALL
    (husband of Regan)**
Dear sir, restrain your rage!»   160

KENT
Kill your physician and then pass his fee
On to the foul disease. Withdraw your gifts,
Or while my throat can still ring out alarms,
I'll tell you "You do evil."

LEAR
                    Hear me, traitor!
Show your allegiance, hear me!—   165

            [KENT kneels]

Since you have sought to make me break my vow—
Which I would never dare—and with forced pride
Have worked to block the discharge of my judgments—
Something my rank and nature can't abide,
My power now disposed, take your reward.   170
Five days I will allow you to prepare
To shield yourself from hardships in this world,
But on the sixth you'll turn your hated back
Upon my kingdom. If, on the tenth day following,
Your banished torso's found in my dominions,   175
That moment is your death. Be gone! By Jupiter,
This shall not be revoked.

KENT
[pausing] Farewell, king. Since you choose to show this
    face,

Freedom lives elsewhere, banished from this place.
[to Cordelia] And pray the gods will shelter you, dear
　　maid,　　　　　　　　　　　　　　　　　　　　　　180
Whose thoughts are just and candidly displayed!
[to Regan and Goneril] And may your actions prove your
　　speeches true,
That from your words of love good deeds ensue.
So Kent, O princes, bids you all adieu.
He'll seek the old ways in a country new.　　　　　　185

　　　　　　　　　　[Exit]

　　[Trumpet fanfare. Re-enter GLOUCESTER, with
　　　FRANCE, BURGUNDY, and ATTENDANTS]

GLOUCESTER
Here's France and Burgundy, my noble lord.

LEAR
My Lord of Burgundy,
I will address you first, who with this king [indicating
　　France]
Vies for my daughter's hand. What is the least
You will require in dowry given outright　　　　　　　190
Before you cease this quest for love.

BURGUNDY (Duke of Burgundy, suitor to Cordelia)
　　　　　　　　　　　　　　　Your majesty,
I seek no more than what your highness offered,
Nor will you offer less.

LEAR
　　　　　　　　　　Most noble Burgundy,
When prized by me, I held her at that value,
But now her worth has dropped. Sir, there she stands.　195
If any of this insubstantial figure,
Or all of it, with my displeasure added,
And nothing more, seems pleasing to your grace,
She's there, and she is yours.

BURGUNDY
                  I've no reply.

LEAR
Will you, with these deficiencies she owns,
Made friendless, now adopted by my hate,
Bequeathed my curses, cast out with my oath,
Take her or leave her?

BURGUNDY
                  Pardon me, royal sir,
But such conditions offer little choice.

LEAR
Then leave her, sir, for by the power that made me,
I've tallied for you all her wealth. [to France] Great king,
I do not wish to lead your love astray
And wed it to my hate. I beg you then
To set your fondness on a worthier course
Than on this wretch whom even nature seems
Ashamed to call her own.

FRANCE (King of France, suitor to Cordelia)
                  So strange that she,
A salve for aging bones, the object that
You're centered on, the focus of your praise,
Your best, your dearest, could in this wink of time
Commit an act so monstrous as to strip
Away all folds of favor. If her offense
Is not unnatural enough as to
Repulse us, then your former, pledged affection
Must now seem suspect. Thinking this of her
Requires a faith that nothing short of miracle
Could ever plant in me.

CORDELIA
While there's still time, I beg your majesty—
Given I lack that glib and oily art
To speak without intent to act, since what I pledge,
I do before I speak—to make it known

That it's no stain of vice, murder, or malice,
No unchaste action or dishonest move,
That has deprived me of your grace and favor.
What I don't have has made me all the richer—
An always-hustling eye, a tongue to match, 230
I'm glad I don't have these—yet lacking them
Has cast me from your liking.

LEAR
                     Better you
Had not been born than not to've pleased me better.

FRANCE
Is it just this—a natural reticence
Which often leaves the actions unannounced 235
That she intends to take? My lord of Burgundy,
What are you saying to her? Love's not love
When it is mingled with concerns that fly
Beyond the central point. Will you have her?
She is herself a dowry.

BURGUNDY
                     Royal king, 240
Just give the payment that you have proposed,
And I will take Cordelia by the hand,
Duchess of Burgundy.

LEAR
Nothing. I've sworn it. I am firm.

BURGUNDY
I'm sorry, then, that having lost a father 245
You too must lose a husband.

CORDELIA
                    Peace be with Burgundy!
Because concerns of wealth comprise his love,
I shall not be his wife.

FRANCE
Fairest Cordelia, who's most rich when poor,
Most chosen when refused, loved when despised— 250
You and your virtues I will seize them here:
The law will let us take what's thrown away.
Gods, gods! It's strange that such a cold neglect
Ignites my love with feverish respect.
Your dowerless daughter, tossed into my hands, 255
Is queen of us, of ours, and our fair France.
Not all the dukes of watery Burgundy
Could buy this low-priced, precious maid I see.
My queen, leave this unnaturalness behind.
Though you've lost here, a better place you'll find. 260

LEAR
You take her, France. Let her be yours, for we
Have no such daughter and shall never see
That face of hers again. [to Cordelia] So now go forth
Without our love, our blessing, or support.—
Come, noble Burgundy. 265

[Flourish. Exit LEAR, BURGUNDY, CORNWALL, AL-
BANY, GLOUCESTER, and ATTENDANTS]

FRANCE
Bid farewell to your sisters.

CORDELIA
Jewels of our father, with these tear-washed eyes
Cordelia leaves you. I see now what you are,
But, as a sister, am quite loath to call
Your faults by their true names. Love father well. 270
To your supposèd bosoms I commit him.
But if, alas, I still stood in his grace,
I'd recommend he seek a better place.
So, farewell to you both.

REGAN
Do not prescribe our duties.

GONERIL
                        Turn your thoughts   275
To pleasing France, who took you in like beggars
Take alms. With your obedience now so slack,
You well deserve to want what you now lack.

CORDELIA
Time will unfold what layers of cunning hide:
Those who mask faults, in time shame must deride.   280
And may you prosper well!

FRANCE
                 Come, fair Cordelia.

[Exit FRANCE and CORDELIA]

GONERIL
Sister, there's much I have to say about what most intimately concerns us both. It seems our father will depart from here tonight.

REGAN
That's most certain, and with you; next month with us.   285

GONERIL
Look how full of impulse his old age is. The observations we have made of this have not been few. He always loved our sister most, and the poor judgment he displayed here in casting her out is only too obvious.

REGAN
It is, no doubt, the infirmities of his age, yet he has ever so   290
slenderly known himself.

GONERIL
Even in his best and soundest years he was rash; thus, we must expect to receive from his age not merely the imperfections of a deeply-embedded disposition but also an unruly wrong-headedness that the infirmity and irritability of his   295
years bring with them.

REGAN
It's likely that Kent's banishment is not the last of these impulsive fits and starts.

GONERIL
There are further formalities of leave-taking between France and him. I hope you'll let us join forces on this. If our father can exercise authority in the manner he just demonstrated, this just-concluded "surrender" of his power can only harm us. 300

REGAN
We shall continue thinking about it.

GONERIL
We must do something while the iron's in the fire. 305

[Exit]

Scene Two. A Hall in Gloucester's Castle

[Enter EDMUND with a letter]

EDMUND
You, nature, are my goddess. To your law
My services are bound. For why should I
Endure the plague of custom and thus let
The legal niceties of states deprive me
Because I trail a brother by some twelve 5
Or fourteen moons. Why bastard? Why debased?
When my physique is just as well composed,
My mind as noble, and my shape the same
As lawful wives bring forth? Why brand us then
As base? With baseness? Bastardly? Debased? 10
Don't we from stealthy acts of natural lust
Receive more character and fiery vigor
Than comes from all the dull, stale, tired beds

That go to make whole tribes of fools conceived
Between the time we sleep and wake? Well then, 15
Legitimate Edgar, I must have your land.
Our father loves the bastard son as much
As the legitimate. Fine word—legitimate!
Well, my legitimate, if this letter works,
And if my scheme goes well, Edmund the base 20
Tops the legitimate. I grow. I prosper.
Now, gods, stand up for bastards!

[Enter GLOUCESTER]

GLOUCESTER
Kent banished outright? France departs in anger?
And the king leaves tonight? His power curbed?
Restricted to a stipend? All this spurred 25
By one sharp jab?—Ah, Edmund! Any news?

EDMUND
There's none your lordship. [hiding the letter]

GLOUCESTER
Why do you so eagerly seek to conceal that letter?

EDMUND
I know of no news, my lord.

GLOUCESTER
What paper were you reading? 30

EDMUND
Nothing, my lord.

GLOUCESTER
No? Then why did you pocket it in such fearful haste? The nature of nothing is such that it has no need to hide itself. Let's see. Come, if it is nothing, I will not need spectacles.

EDMUND
I beg you, sir, spare me from showing you. It is a letter 35

from my brother that I have not finished, but what I have perused so far is not, I find, suitable for you to read.

GLOUCESTER
Give me the letter, sir.

EDMUND
I will offend you whether I retain it or give it up. The contents, as far as I understand them, are blameworthy.

GLOUCESTER
Let's see, let's see!

EDMUND
I hope my brother's rationale for writing this was merely to assess or test my virtue.

GLOUCESTER
[reads] *"This contrived practice of revering the aged turns the world bitter during our prime and keeps our wealth from us till our old bones cannot relish it. I am finding that this tyrannical oppression by the aged is merely a useless, foolish servitude. It holds sway not because of its power but because of our acquiescence. Come see me so I can speak more of this. If I were to control when our father awoke, you would enjoy half his income forever and be loved by your brother,*
—*Edgar."*

Hum! Conspiracy?—"Control when our father awoke—you would enjoy half his income."—My son Edgar! Could his hand write this? Could his heart and brain brew this? When did you receive this? Who brought it?

EDMUND
It was not brought to me, my lord—that's the cunning of it. It was tossed through the window of my bedroom.

GLOUCESTER
You're sure the handwriting is your brother's?

EDMUND
If the message had been noble, my lord, I'd swear it was his, but given the content, I'd prefer to think it is not.

GLOUCESTER
It is his.

EDMUND
It is his hand, my lord, but I hope his heart is not in the contents. 65

GLOUCESTER
Has he ever approached you before with this business?

EDMUND
Never, my lord, but I've often heard him maintain that it is appropriate when sons reach maturity and fathers are in decline for the father to be the ward of the son and for the son to manage his estate. 70

GLOUCESTER
O villain, villain!—That very opinion in this letter! Abhorrent villain!—Unnatural, detestable, brutish villain! Worse than brutish! Go, young man, seek him. I'll apprehend him. Abominable villain! Where is he?

EDMUND
I am not certain, my lord. If it is your decision to delay your indignation against my brother until you can draw from him a clearer declaration of his intent, then you should keep on a safe course; whereas, if you aggressively proceed against him and misjudge his purpose, it will leave a great breach in your own reputation and shatter into pieces the heart of his obedience. I would stake my life that he wishes to test whether I harbor animosity toward you and has no malicious intent beyond that. 75

80

GLOUCESTER
You think so?

EDMUND
If your honor judges it proper, I will place you where you will be able to hear us confer on this, and with this verbal verification, you'll have confirmation, barring further delay, no later than this evening.

GLOUCESTER
He cannot be such a monster.

⟨**EDMUND**
And surely is not.

GLOUCESTER
To his father, who so tenderly and entirely loves him. Heaven and earth!⟩ Edmund, seek him out; in my behalf, cozy up to him. Manage this business according to your judgment. I would forfeit my rank to resolve these doubts.

EDMUND
I will seek him, sir, at once, carry out this business as appropriate, and report the outcome.

GLOUCESTER
These eclipses of the sun and moon of late do not portend well for us. Natural science can explain them as being this or that, yet nature finds itself scourged by the effects that follow: love cools, friendship counts for nothing, brothers feud; in cities, rebellion; in countries, discord; in palaces, treason; and bonds cracked between son and father. ⟪This villain I've spawned falls under this ill omen: there's son against father; the king rubs against nature's grain; there's father against child. We have seen the best of our times. Now machinations, deceit, treachery, and ruinous misdeeds will follow us unquietly to our graves.⟫ Expose this villain, Edmund, and you will lose nothing by it. Do it carefully. And the noble and true-hearted Kent banished! His offence, honesty! It's strange.

[Exit]

EDMUND
So tremendous is the foolishness in this world that when our prospects sicken—often from the excesses of our own behavior—we lay blame for our disasters on the sun, the moon, and the stars, as if we were villains by necessity, fools by heavenly compulsion, knaves, thieves, and traitors by celestial predestination, drunkards, liars, and adulterers by an enforced obedience to planetary influence, and all our evil done through divine provocation. An astonishing evasion for these whoring men to blame their goatish disposition on the authority of some star! My father coupled with my mother under the tail of some astral dragon and the blessed event of my birth took place under Ursa Major, so it follows that I am brash and lecherous. Puh! I would have been what I am if the star of chastity itself had twinkled on this bastard's making.   115   120   125

[Enter EDGAR]

On cue! He arrives, like the climax in an old comedy. My part calls for severe melancholy, with the sighs of a panhandling lunatic. [aloud] O, these eclipses do foretell of this discord! Fa, sol, la, mi. [hums off tune]

EDGAR (son of Gloucester)
Hello there, brother Edmund! What serious contemplation are you engaged in?   130

EDMUND
I am thinking, brother, about a prediction I read the other day of what might follow these eclipses.

EDGAR
Do you busy yourself with that?

EDMUND
I assure you the consequences he writes of conclude unhappily: ⟨unnatural disharmony between child and parent, death, famine, dissolution of ancient allegiances, divisions   135

in the state, curses and maledictions against kings and nobles, groundless distrust, banishment of friends, desertion of troops, nuptial breaches, and I know not what.

EDGAR
How long have you been a disciple of astrology?

EDMUND
Tell me,⟩ when did you see my father last?

EDGAR
Just last night.

EDMUND
Did you speak with him?

EDGAR
Yes, for two hours.

EDMUND
Did you part on good terms? Did you sense any displeasure in his voice or manner?

EDGAR
None at all.

EDMUND
Think back on how you might have offended him. And I urge you to avoid his presence for just a bit so time can lessen the intensity of his displeasure, which at this instant rages so much inside him that even physical injury to you would not diminish it.

EDGAR
Some villain has done me wrong.

EDMUND
That's my fear. ⟪I beg you to restrain yourself from approaching him until his rage slows. Now listen carefully. Stay with me in my lodgings until the time is right for you

to speak with my lord. Please, go. Here's my key. If you do
go out, go armed.

EDGAR
Armed, brother?» 160

EDMUND
Brother, that's my best advice. I'd be a dishonest man if I
saw anything but malice here. I have told you what I have
seen and heard—but softened it—not even close to the true
horror of it all. Please go.

EDGAR
Will I hear from you soon? 165

EDMUND
I'll take care of this business for you.

[Exit EDGAR]

A credulous father and a noble brother,
Whose nature is so far from doing harm
That he suspects none, on whose foolish trust
My schemes so easily ride! The way's now clear. 170
Let me, if not by birth, gain land through craft.
For any means that works to me seems apt.

[Exit]

Scene Three. A Room in Albany's Palace

[Enter GONERIL and OSWALD]

GONERIL
Did my father strike my steward [referring to Oswald] for
chiding his fool?

OSWALD (steward to Goneril)
Yes, madam.

GONERIL
All day and night he wrongs me. Every hour
He bounds from one offense to one more flagrant 5
And puts us all at odds. I won't endure it.
His knights are rowdy, and his "highness" scolds us
For every trifle. When he returns from hunting,
I will not speak with him. Say I am sick.
And if your former service to him slackens, 10
You're doing well, and I will answer for you.

OSWALD
[horns within] He's coming, madam. I hear him.

GONERIL
Display a drowsy negligence as suits
You and your staff. I want to force the issue.
If he dislikes it, let him see my sister. 15
Her mind and mine, I know, are one in this
⟨And won't be overruled. Senseless old man
Who still expects to wield authority
That he just gave away!—I swear by God,
Old fools are babes again, so we must praise 20
As well as discipline him when he strays.⟩⁴
Remember what I've said.

OSWALD
      Very well, madam

GONERIL
And let his knights grow colder toward your staff.
What comes of it—advise them not to worry.
⟨I know these instances will breed a chance 25
To scold him.⟩ I'll write my sister right away
To hold to this same course. Prepare for dinner.

      [Exit]

Scene Four. A Hall in Albany's Palace

[Enter KENT, disguised and beardless]

KENT (masquerading as Caius)
If I'm as good at borrowing an accent
And can disguise my speech, the worthy goal
For which I have erased my outer form
May yet be realized. Now, banished Kent,
If you can serve where you now stand condemned, 5
Then it may happen, that this king you love,
Will find a tireless servant.

[Horns within. Enter KING LEAR,
KNIGHTS, and ATTENDANTS]

LEAR
I won't wait a second for dinner. Go get it ready.

[Exit an ATTENDANT]

And who do we have here?

KENT
A man, sir. 10

LEAR
What is your profession? What do you wish from us?

KENT
I profess to be no less than what I seem, to serve whoever
truly confides in me, to love whoever's honest, to associate
with whoever's wise and says little, to fear God's judgment,
to fight when I have no other choice, and to refuse to eat fish. 15

LEAR
What are you?

KENT
A very honest-hearted fellow, and as poor as the king.

LEAR
If you are as poor a subject as he is a king, you are certainly poor. What do you want?

KENT
To serve.

LEAR
Who do you wish to serve?

KENT
You.

LEAR
Do you know who I am, man?

KENT
No, sir, but your bearing has something for which I would gladly call you master.

LEAR
What's that?

KENT
Authority.

LEAR
What service can you provide?

KENT
I can maintain confidentiality, ride, run, spoil an elaborate tale in the telling of it, yet deliver a plain message bluntly. Whatever ordinary men are suited for, I am qualified to do, and I'm most noted for my diligence.

LEAR
How old are you?

KENT
Not so young, sir, that I'd love a woman only for her singing and not so old as to worship only her presence. I have forty-eight years on my back.

LEAR
Follow me. You shall serve me. If I like you no worse after dinner, I will not take leave of you yet.—Dinner, ho, dinner! Where's my boy? My fool? Go and call my fool in here.

[Exit an ATTENDANT]
[Enter OSWALD]

You, you, fellow, where's my daughter? 40

OSWALD
Please excuse me—

[Exit]

LEAR
What did that fellow say? Call that numbskull back.

[Exit a KNIGHT]

Where's my fool, ho? I think the world's asleep.

[Re-enter KNIGHT]

What? You're back? Where is that mongrel?

KNIGHT
He says, my lord, that your daughter is not well. 45

LEAR
Why didn't that slave come back to me when I called him?

KNIGHT
Sir, he told me in the rudest manner that he does not wish to.

LEAR
He does not wish to?

KNIGHT
My lord, I do not know what the matter is, but in my judgment your highness is not being treated with the courtly 50 respect to which you are accustomed. A great diminishing of respect has appeared in the household staff as well as in the duke himself and your daughter.

LEAR
Ha! Is that what you say?

KNIGHT
I beg your forgiveness, my lord, if I am mistaken, but it's my duty to speak out when I think your highness has been wronged.

LEAR
You have done no more than remind me of my own thoughts. I have perceived a rather lackadaisical neglect of late that I have owed more to my own heightened sensitivity than to any deliberate intent or aim to show ingratitude. I will look further into it. But where's my fool? I have not seen him for two days.

KNIGHT
Since the young lady left for France, sir, the fool has been pining away.

LEAR
No more about that. I am well aware of that. Go now and tell my daughter I wish to speak with her.

[Exit ATTENDANT]

Go now, and call my fool in here.

[Exit another ATTENDANT]
[Re-enter OSWALD]

O you, sir. You, come over here. Who am I, sir?

OSWALD
My lady's father.

LEAR
"My lady's father?" My lord's errand-boy, you son of a whore! You slave! You mutt!

OSWALD
I am none of those, my lord. I beg your pardon.

LEAR
Are you volleying looks with me, you scoundrel? [striking him]

OSWALD
I'm not a ball to be struck, my lord. 75

KENT
Nor tripped, you lowlife shagger of them. [tripping him by the heels]

LEAR
I thank you, fellow. Serve me well, and you'll see favors.

KENT
[to Oswald] Come, sir, get up and be gone. I'll teach you to distinguish rank. Out, out! If you want me to lay out and measure your oafish length again, then linger. Otherwise 80 be gone! Out, if you have any sense.

[Pushes OSWALD out].

So there.

LEAR
Now, my friendly fellow, I thank you. Take this advance for your services. [giving Kent money]

[Enter FOOL]

FOOL (Lear's Fool)
Let me hire him too. Here's my fool's cap. 85

[Giving KENT his rooster-combed cap]

LEAR
Ah, my little knave! How are you?

FOOL
Fellow, you had best take my cap.

KENT
Why, fool?

FOOL
Why, for taking up with what is out of favor. No, if you can't smile into the wind, you'll soon be out in the cold. Here, take my fool's cap. This fellow, despite desires to the contrary, has banished two of his daughters and done the third a favor. If you follow him, you will have to wear my cap.—Greetings, uncle! If only I had two fool's caps and two daughters!

LEAR
Why, my boy?

FOOL
If I gave them all my possessions, I could still keep my fool's caps for myself. Here's mine. Beg your daughters for another.

LEAR
Take heed, fellow—of the whip.

FOOL
Truth's a dog sent to the kennel. He's whipped and sent outside, while the lady hound may sit by the fire and stink.

LEAR
A pestilent irritant to me!

FOOL
Fellow, I'll teach you a rhyme.

LEAR
Do.

FOOL
Mark this, uncle:—
Show less than you own,
Say less than is known,
Owe more than you loan,
Use less than you've grown,
Bet less on what's shown,
See more than is thrown;

Leave your drink and your whores,
And stay home indoors,
And then you'll have plenty
Three tens for each twenty.

KENT
This means nothing, fool.

FOOL
Then it is like breath from an unpaid lawyer—you gave me nothing for it. Can you make any use of nothing, uncle?

LEAR
Why, no, boy. Nothing can be made out of nothing.

FOOL
[to Kent] Please tell him then how much the rent of his land comes to. He will not believe a fool.

LEAR
Bitter words, fool!

FOOL
Do you know the difference, my boy, between a bitter fool and a sweet one?

LEAR
No, lad, teach me.

FOOL
⟨*The lord that counseled thee*
  To give your land away,
Come place him here by me—
  It's his role that you'll play.
The sweet and bitter fools
  Will now be made distinct;
The first's in motley here,
  The other's there I think. [pointing at Lear]

LEAR
Are you calling me a fool, boy?

FOOL
You have given all your other titles away, the ones you were born with. 135

KENT
There's more here than his foolishness, my lord.

FOOL
Yes, by God. Lords and great men won't let me have it all. If I had a monopoly on it, they would take a piece and the ladies would too. They would not let me keep my piece to 140
myself [indicating a bauble he's wearing]. They'd snatch at it.⟩—Uncle, give me an egg, and I'll give you two crowns.

LEAR
And where would you get these crowns?

FOOL
Why, after I have cut the egg down the middle and eaten the insides, I'd have the two crowns of the egg. When you 145
slice your crown down the middle and give away both parts, you are bearing your jackass on your back through the dirt. You had little sense in your bald crown when you gave your golden one away. If I speak out like a fool in saying this, why not whip the one who first saw that it was so. 150

[singing] *Fools are less in vogue this season,*
  For the wise are fooled by gimmickry,
Not knowing how to wear their reason,
  Like apes, they go for mimicry.

LEAR
Since when have you been so full of songs, my man? 155

FOOL
I've made it my habit, uncle, ever since you turned your daughters into your mothers—when you gave them the rod and dropped your own pants—

[singing] *Their eyes soon filled with joyous dew,*

> *While I sang mournful tunes,* 160
> *That such a king plays peek-a-boo*
> *And goes among buffoons.*

Please, uncle, hire a schoolmaster who can teach your fool to lie. I would gladly learn to lie.

LEAR
If you lie, my friend, I'll have you whipped. 165

FOOL
I marvel at what close kin you and your daughters are. They'll have me whipped for speaking the truth, you'll have me for whipped for lying, and sometimes I am whipped for holding my peace. I'd rather be anything but a fool. And yet I don't wish to be you, uncle. You've sliced off pieces of 170 your reason on both sides and left nothing in the middle. Here comes one of the slices.

[Enter GONERIL]

LEAR
Greetings, daughter? Why such a face? Lately it seems that you frown too much.

FOOL
You were a pretty fellow when you had no need to care about 175 her frowning. Now you're a zero without a number in front of it. I am more than you are. I am a fool, you are nothing. [to Goneril] Yes, I swear, I will hold my tongue. Your face tells me to, though you say nothing.

> *Mum, mum,* 180
> *He who keeps no crust or crumb,*
> *Weary of it, soon needs some.—*

[pointing to Lear] That's an empty pea pod.

GONERIL
Not only him, sir, your uncensored fool,
But others in your insolent retinue 185

Constantly carp and quarrel, breaking out
In gross, intolerable outbursts. Sir,
I'd thought, by making this well known to you,
I'd found a surefire cure, but now grow fearful,
Considering all you've lately said and done,
That you defend these acts and goad them on
Through your approval. Do this and these wrongs
Won't bypass blame and remedies won't sleep,
Which, to maintain a peaceful, healthy state,
Might, when applied, cause harm to you in ways
Which may seem shameful but necessity
Will deem a prudent course.

FOOL
As you know, uncle,

> *The sparrow fed the cuckoo for so long*
> *Its head got bit off by its young.*

So out went the candle, and we were left in darkness.

LEAR
Are you my daughter?

GONERIL
Come, sir,
I wish you'd make some use of that good judgment
I know is stored in you—and put away
This frame of mind that has of late transformed you
From what you truly are.

FOOL
Doesn't even a donkey know when the cart is drawing the horse?—[sings] *Whoops, tart! I love you!*

LEAR
Does no one here know me?—This is not Lear.
Is this Lear's walk? His voice? Where are his eyes?
Either his mind has weakened, or his senses
Lulled into sleep. —Awake? I can't be. No!—
Who is it that can tell me who I am?

FOOL
Lear's shadow.   215

⟨**LEAR**
[perhaps ignoring the Fool]
I want to learn. These tokens of my sovereignty,
Knowledge, and common sense persuade me falsely
That I'm a man with daughters.

FOOL
Whom they'll turn into a well-trained father.⟩

LEAR
Your name, fair gentlewoman?   220

GONERIL
This sham surprise is much in keeping with
Your other recent pranks. And I must urge you
To understand exactly my intent.
Old and revered, you also should be wise.
Here you still keep a hundred knights and squires,   225
Men so disorderly, depraved, and brash
That this, our court, infected with their manners,
Is more a rowdy inn. This gluttony and lust
Make it more like a tavern or a brothel
Than honored palace. Shame alone demands   230
An instant remedy. One thus requests,
One who will otherwise demand what's asked,
A slight reduction in your entourage,
And those who do continue under you
Will be such men as may befit your age,   235
Who know their role and you.

LEAR
                    Darkness and devils
Saddle my horses. Call my train together.—
Degenerate bastard! I won't deal with you.
There's still one daughter left.

GONERIL
You strike my people. And your unruly rabble
Makes servants of their betters.

[Enter ALBANY]

LEAR
Woe to those who repent too late!—[to Albany] You're
  here, sir?
Is it your wish? Speak sir.—Prepare my horses.—
Ingratitude, you marble-hearted fiend,
More hideous when you surface in a child
Than monsters from the sea!

«ALBANY
                    Please, sir, be calm.»

LEAR
[to Goneril] Detested buzzard, how you lie!
My knights, all from the choicest, rarest cuts,
Know well the finest points of all their duties,
And with exacting diligence uphold
The honor of their name. So small a fault,
You looked so ugly in Cordelia!
Like some machine, you wrenched my natural frame
From its foundation, drained my heart of love,
And swelled this bitterness. O Lear, Lear, Lear!
Beat at this gate that let your folly in [strikes his head]
And precious judgment out! Go, go, my people.

ALBANY
My lord, I'm guiltless, as I'm ignorant
«Of what's provoked you.»

LEAR
                    It may be so, my lord.
Hear, nature, hear. Dear goddess, hear!
Suspend these goings on if you intend
To make this creature fruitful!
Into her womb convey sterility!
Dry up the organs of her procreation,

And from her debased body never spring 265
A babe to honor her! If she must breed,
Create a child from spite so it may live
To be a trying, aberrant torment to her!
Let it stamp wrinkles on her youthful brow,
With running tears carve channels in her cheeks, 270
Repay maternal labor and attention
With mockery and contempt, so she may feel
How so much sharper than a serpent's tooth
It is to have a thankless child!—Away!

[Exit]

ALBANY
Oh, gods that we adore, what's prompted this? 275

GONERIL
Don't give a thought to any more of this
But just allow his moods the latitude
Senility affords.

[Re-enter LEAR]

LEAR
What, fifty of my followers at a stroke!
Within a fortnight!

ALBANY
                What's the matter, sir? 280

LEAR
I'll tell you.—Life and death!—[to Goneril] I am ashamed
You have the power to shake my manhood so
And force hot tears from me as if you could
Be worthy of them.—Blights and plagues on you!
May unstitched gashes of a father's curse 285
Pierce you in every sense!—Old foolish eyes,
Weep over this again, I'll pluck you out
And use you and the liquid that you lose
To soften clay. It's come to this? Then, ha!
Let it be so. I have another daughter 290

Who, I am sure, is kind and comforting.
When she gets word of all this, with her nails
She'll flay your wolfish visage. You will find
That I'll resume the role which you now think
I have cast off forever.

[Exit LEAR, KENT, and ATTENDANTS]

GONERIL
Did you hear that? 295

ALBANY
I must not be too biased, Goneril,
By this great love I have for you—

GONERIL
Please, don't concern yourself.—What, Oswald, ho!
[to the Fool] You, sir, more rogue than fool, go after him.

FOOL
Uncle Lear, Uncle Lear, hold on—take your foolishness 300
with you.—
A fox when one has caught her,
And such a daughter,
Would have met their slaughter,
If my cap had somehow shot her 305
Instead I run like water.

[Exit]

GONERIL
«This man has been well-staffed.—A hundred knights!
It's prudent and it's safe to let him keep
A hundred ready knights. Right, so at every itch,
Each whim, each murmur, each complaint, dislike, 310
He'll safeguard his senescence with their power—
Our lives held at his mercy.—Oswald, I say!—

ALBANY
Your fears may go too far.

GONERIL
Safer than trust too far.
It's better to remove the harms I fear   315
Than fear I'll be removed. I know his heart.
What he has said I relayed to my sister.
If she maintains him and his hundred knights,
Once I have shown the mess it's made—»

[Re-enter OSWALD]

                              Oh, Oswald!
Well, did you write that letter to my sister?   320

OSWALD
Yes, madam.

GONERIL
You'll need an escort, and go there by horse.
Inform her fully of my private fears,
And toss in any reasons of your own
That may support it more. Get going now   325
And rush back here at once.

[Exit OSWALD]

                            No, no, my lord!
This yielding, gentle manner of behavior,
I won't condemn it, yet, if you'll forgive me,
You will earn greater blame for lack of prudence
Than praise for risking mildness.   330

ALBANY
How far your eyes may pierce I cannot tell.
Striving for better, oft we mar what's well.

GONERIL
Not this time.

ALBANY
Well, well, we shall see.

[Exit]

Scene Five. The Court before Albany's Palace

[Enter LEAR, KENT, and FOOL]

LEAR
Go ahead of me to Gloucester County with this letter. Reveal to my daughter no more than whatever questions this letter prompts her to ask you. If you're not speedy in its delivery, I will be there before you.

KENT
I will not sleep, my lord, till I have delivered your letter. 5

[Exit]

FOOL
[tired from walking] If a man thought with his feet, wouldn't his brain be in danger of frostbite?

LEAR
Yes, boy.

FOOL
Then cheer up. Your brain's a safe distance from yours.

LEAR
Ha, ha, ha! 10

FOOL
Look forward to the same treatment from your other daughter, for she's as close to this one as crab is to apple, and I mean what I mean.

LEAR
What's that, boy?

FOOL
That these two differ in taste no more than two crab apples 15 do. Can you tell me why one's nose is in the middle o' one's face?

LEAR
No.

FOOL
Why, to keep one's eyes on either side, so whatever a man cannot sniff out, he may still peer into. 20

LEAR
I have done her wrong.

FOOL
Can you tell how an oyster makes his shell?

LEAR
No.

FOOL
Me neither, but I can tell why a snail has a house.

LEAR
Why? 25

FOOL
Why, to put his head in—not to give it away to his daughters and leave his horns exposed.

LEAR
I'll abandon my natural role. So kind a father!—Are my horses ready?

FOOL
Your asses have gone after them. The reason why the seven 30 sisters has only seven stars is an ingenious reason.

LEAR
Because there are not eight?

FOOL
Yes indeed. You would make a good fool.

LEAR
To take it back through force!—Monstrous ingratitude!

FOOL
If you were my fool, uncle, I'd have you beaten for being old   35
before your time.

LEAR
How's that?

FOOL
You should not have been old till you had been wise.

LEAR
O, let me not be mad, not mad, sweet heaven!
Keep my composure. I don't wish for madness!—   40

[Enter a GENTLEMAN]

Here we are. Are the horses ready?

GENTLEMAN
Ready, my lord.

LEAR
Come, boy.

FOOL
If she's a virgin still,
And laughs when I depart her,   45
She won't be one for long,
Unless this thing's cut shorter.

[Exit]

King Lear

Act Two

Act Two

Scene One. Court Within Gloucester's Castle

[Enter EDMUND and CURAN, meeting]

EDMUND
Good day, Curan.

CURAN (a gentleman in the Gloucester Household)
And you, sir. I have been with your father and have informed him that the Duke of Cornwall and Regan, his duchess, will be here with him tonight.

EDMUND
What brought this about? 5

CURAN
I cannot say. Have you heard the talk going around? I mean the whispered part, for these reports are still only light kisses to the ear.

EDMUND
No, I haven't. Please, go on.

CURAN
You haven't heard of likely wars looming between the dukes 10
of Cornwall and Albany?

EDMUND
Not a word.

CURAN
You may hear of it soon enough. Farewell, sir.

[Exit]

EDMUND
The Duke comes here tonight? So much the better.
This weaves itself no doubt into my business.
My father's told the guard to seize my brother,
And I have one thing, of a delicate nature,
That I must finish. Speed and luck may help!—
Brother, a word! Down here. Brother, I say!

[Enter EDGAR]

Our father's watching. O sir, flee this place.
Informants have revealed where you are hid.
You now can take advantage of the night.—
Did you speak out against the Duke of Cornwall?
He's coming here— right now, tonight, and fast,
And Regan's with him. Have you spoken out
Regarding this dispute with Albany?
Think carefully.

EDGAR
        I'm certain, not a word.

EDMUND
I hear my father coming. Pardon me.
This ploy requires I draw my sword on you.
Draw—as if in defense. Play your part well.
Yield! [spoken loudly]. Stand before my father.—Some
    light in here!
[to Edgar] Flee, brother.—[loudly] Torches, torches!—[to
    Edgar] So farewell.

[Exit EDGAR]

Blood drawn from me would foster the illusion
Of a more fierce encounter. [wounds his arm] I've seen
    drunkards
Do more than this in jest.—Father, father!
Stop, stop! Help!

[Enter GLOUCESTER, and SERVANTS with torches]

GLOUCESTER
            We're here, Edmund. Where's the villain?

EDMUND
He stood here in the dark, his sharp sword out,
And mumbled wicked spells, invoked the moon
To be his guardian mistress—

GLOUCESTER
                    But where is he?

EDMUND
Look, sir, I'm bleeding.

GLOUCESTER
                Where's the villain, Edmund?   40

EDMUND
Fled this way, sir. When by no means could he—

GLOUCESTER
Pursue him! After him.

            [Exit SERVANTS]

            —By no means what?

EDMUND
—Persuade me to assassinate your lordship,
But then I told him the avenging Gods
Will turn on patricide with all their thunder   45
And spoke of how a strong and complex bond
Binds children to their father. Finally, sir,
Seeing how loathingly I stood opposed
To his unnatural scheme, in one fierce thrust
His sword unsheathed and ready, he attacked   50
My unprotected body, lanced my arm;
But when he saw my powers at their fullest,
Emboldened by just cause, roused in defense,
Or startled maybe by the noise I made,
Quite suddenly he fled.

GLOUCESTER
>   He'd best flee far,
For in this land he won't remain uncaught
And, once he's found, dispatched. My noble master,
My worthy duke and patron, comes tonight.
By his authority I will proclaim this:
Whoever apprehends this murderous coward
And brings him to the stake deserves our thanks,
He who conceals him, death.

EDMUND
When I advised against this aim of his
And found him resolute, with biting words
I threatened to expose him. He replied,
"You property-less bastard! Realize that,
Were I to contradict you, there's no store
Of trust or worth or virtue placed in you
To make your words believed. No. I'd deny
It all, I would—yes, even if you had
My signed confession, I would make it all
Seem your connivance, plot, and odious scheming.
You'd have to hope the world's filled up with dolts
Who cannot see how profit from my death
Becomes a much too plain and potent spur
To make you seek it."

GLOUCESTER
>   Oh, deviant, hardened villain!
Deny this letter, he said? I never sired him.

[Trumpets within]

Hark, the duke's trumpets! Why's he coming here?
Seal off the ports; the villain won't escape;
The duke must grant me that. And then, his picture—
I'll send it far and near so all the kingdom
Will take due note of him. As for my land,
Loyal and natural boy, I'll find the means
To make you legal heir.

[Enter CORNWALL, REGAN, and ATTENDANTS]

CORNWALL
Greetings, my noble friend! Since I arrived—
Just now, I'd like to add—I've heard strange news.

REGAN
If it is true, all vengeance falls too short
In hounding this offender. Lord, how are you?

GLOUCESTER
O madam, my old heart is cracked—it's cracked!

REGAN
What, did my father's godson seek your life?
The one my father named? Your Edgar?

GLOUCESTER
O lady, lady, shame wants me to hide it!

REGAN
Wasn't he friendly with those rowdy knights
In service to my father?

GLOUCESTER
I don't know, madam. It's all bad, all bad.

EDMUND
Yes, madam, he was part of that assemblage.

REGAN
No marvel then that he grew ill-disposed.
They've prodded him to seek the old man's death,
To take control and plunder his estate.
My sister has, in fact, this very evening
Informed me of them fully, with such warnings
That if it's my house where they plan to stay,
I won't be home.

CORNWALL
          Nor I, believe me, Regan.
Edmund, I hear that you have shown your father
The loyalty of a son.

EDMUND
                Sir, it's my duty.　　　　　　　　　　105

GLOUCESTER
He has exposed the intrigue and received
This wound you see while struggling to arrest him.

CORNWALL
Are they pursuing him?

GLOUCESTER
                Yes, my good lord.

CORNWALL
If he is taken, he won't be a threat
To anyone again. So use my clout　　　　　　　　110
However you may please. As for you, Edmund,
Whose virtuous obedience has just now
Endorsed itself so fully, join with me.
Natures so deeply loyal, I surely need;
You're one I'll grab at once.

EDMUND
                I'll serve you, sir,　　　　115
Faithfully, at the least.

GLOUCESTER
Your grace, I'll thank you for him.

CORNWALL
Do you know why we came to visit you?—

REGAN
—Threading the night's dark eye so out of season.
There's business, noble Gloucester, of some weight　　120
On which we must make use of your advice.
Our father's written, and our sister too,
Of some disputes, which I believe are best
Resolved away from home. These messengers
Await to be dispatched. Our dear old friend,　　　125
Please soothe the wounds felt in your heart and give
Us needed guidance on these matters here,
Which urge a prompt response.

GLOUCESTER
                    I'll serve you, madam.
Your honored presence is quite welcome.

[Flourish]
[Exit]

Scene Two. Outside Gloucester's Castle

[Enter separately KENT (as Caius) and OSWALD]

OSWALD
Good morning, friend. Are you a servant here?

KENT (masquerading as CAIUS)
Yes. [lying]

OSWALD
Where may we rest our horses?

KENT
                    In the bog.

OSWALD
Be kind enough to tell me.

KENT
                    I'm not kind.

OSWALD
Well then, I won't concern myself with you.

5

KENT
If I herded you with my teeth, then you'd show concern for me.

OSWALD
Why do you treat me like this? I don't know you.

KENT
Fellow, I know you.

OSWALD
Who do you take me for?

KENT
A knave, a rascal, an eater of kitchen scraps; a base, vain, shallow, beggarly, three-shirts-to-his-name, wage-earning, filthy, untailored knave; a yellow-bellied, litigation-happy, wretched, mirror-primping, officious, finicky rogue; a one-trunk-owning slave, who would pimp if it were his duty, and is nothing but a mixture of knave, beggar, coward, panderer, and son and heir of a mongrel bitch: one whom I will beat into clamorous whining if you deny even one syllable of these titles I've given you.

OSWALD
Why, what kind of monstrous fellow are you to rail like this at someone who's not known to you nor knows you?

KENT
What a bold-faced scalawag you are to deny you know me! Wasn't it two days ago that I beat you and tripped you in front of the king? Draw, you rogue, for though it's still night, the moon is shining, and I'll sop up the moonlight with you. Draw, you despicable pretty-boy son of a whore. Draw! [draws his sword]

OSWALD
Away! I want nothing to do with you.

KENT
Draw, you rascal. You come with letters against the king and have joined Miss Vanity's puppet show against her father's royalty. Draw, you rogue, or I'll slice up and broil your hindquarters. Draw, you rascal. Get to it!

OSWALD
Help, ho! Murder! Help!

KENT
Fight, you slave! Make a stand, rogue! Fight, you sissy!

[Beating him]

OSWALD
Help, ho! Murder! Murder!

[Enter EDMUND (with his sword drawn), REGAN, CORNWALL, GLOUCESTER, and SERVANTS]

EDMUND
Here now! What's this all about?

KENT
About you, houseboy, if you wish. Come and get a taste of it. Come on, young master.

GLOUCESTER
Weapons? Arms? What's the matter here?

CORNWALL
Cease, if you value life!
He who strikes next must die. Now what's the matter?

REGAN
They're messengers from my sister and the king.

CORNWALL
Why this dispute? Speak.

OSWALD
I am short of breath, my lord.

KENT
No wonder, since you've ignited your courage so. You cowardly rascal, nature wants no credit for you. A tailor made you.

CORNWALL
You are an odd fellow. A tailor made a man?

KENT
Yes, a tailor, sir. A stonecutter or a painter with only two hours of training could not have made him so badly.

CORNWALL
But tell us what prompted this quarrel?

OSWALD
This antiquated ruffian did, sir, whose life I have spared
out of respect for his gray beard—

KENT
Useless son of a whore! You worthless appendage!—My lord,
if you'll allow it, I will trample this unsifted villain into
mortar and plaster the walls of an outhouse with him.—You
spared my gray beard, you quivering wagtail?

CORNWALL
Peace, man!
You savage knave. Have you no reverence?

KENT
Yes, sir, I do. But rage exempts me from it.

CORNWALL
Why are you angry?

KENT
That such a slave as this could wear a sword
Yet wear no honesty. Such smiling rogues as these,
Like rats, they gnaw through cords of holy union
Too knotted to untie, massage the lust
Rebelling in the hearts of their superiors;
Add oil to fire, snow to their colder moods;
Deny, affirm, and turn like weather vanes
With every gust and shifting of their masters,
Like dogs, know nothing, but to follow.
A plague upon your snide, misshapen grimace!
Smile at my speech, as if I am a jester?
Goose, if you had a swamp in which to swim,
I'd drive you cackling home to shiver in it.[1]

CORNWALL
What, are you mad, old fellow?

GLOUCESTER
What caused this quarrel? Tell us.   75

KENT
No opposites are less compatible
Than such a knave and I.

CORNWALL
But why call him a knave? What's his offense?

KENT
His face displeases me.

CORNWALL
No more perhaps than mine, or his, or hers.   80

KENT
Sir, it's my disposition to be blunt.
I have seen better faces in my time
Than those that rest on any neck I see
In front of me this moment.

CORNWALL
                    Quite a fellow,
Who, praising his own frankness, then puts on   85
A bratty roughness and thus robs the style
Of its true role. He cannot flatter us—
His frank and honest mind must speak the truth!
If we accept it, fine; if not, he's frank.
I know this kind of knave whose honest speech   90
Can harbor more corrupt and cunning schemes
Than twenty silly, fawning, mindlessly
Attentive sycophants.

KENT
[adopting a courtly manner] Sir, in good faith, in sincere
    truthfulness,
Under kind rule from your celestial perch,   95
Whose influence, like the wreath of radiant fire
That flickers on the Sun God's brow—

CORNWALL
                              What's this?

KENT
I'm shedding the manner that you objected to so much. Sir,
I know I'm no flatterer. Whoever deceived you with plain
speech was a plain knave, something I won't be, even if my   100
refusal earns your disapproval.[2]

CORNWALL
What's the nature of your offense?

OSWALD
I have committed none.
He pleased the king, his master, recently
By striking me when he misunderstood me;   105
In league with him, and nursing his ill-feeling,
He tripped me from behind. I'm down, I'm scorned,
Insulted, while he showed enough bravado
To earn himself the praises of the king
For taking on one who did not resist.   110
And flushed with triumph from this dreadful exploit
He drew on me again.

KENT
                    These rogues and cowards
Think all the brave are fools.[3]

CORNWALL
                           Go fetch the stocks!—
You brash and ancient knave, you "honored" braggart,
We'll teach you—

KENT
                 Sir, I am too old to learn.   115
Don't fetch your stocks for me. I serve the king,
In whose employment I was sent to you.
You will show scant respect, ill-will too bold
Against the crown and honor of my master,
If you abuse his messenger.   120

CORNWALL
Go fetch the stocks! As I have life and honor,
There he shall sit till noon.

REGAN
Till noon! Till night, my lord, and all night too!

KENT
Why, madam, if I were your father's dog,
You would not treat me so.

REGAN
                    Since you're his knave, I will.   125

CORNWALL
This is a fellow of that very stripe
My sister speaks of.—Come, bring out the stocks!

      [Stocks brought out]

GLOUCESTER
Your grace, let me implore you not to do this.
⟨He's much at fault, and the good king, his master,
Will censure him. But this demeaning sentence   130
Is what the lowest, most despised of wretches,
What thieves and other common criminals
Are punished with.⟩ The king will see a slight
If his own envoy is so little honored
That he's restrained like this.

CORNWALL
                    I'll answer for it.   135

      [KENT is put in the stocks]

REGAN
My sister may respond to this much worse,
To have her gentleman abused, assaulted,
⟨For acting on her orders.—Put in his legs.⟩
Come, my good lord, away.

[Exit all but GLOUCESTER and KENT]

GLOUCESTER
I'm sorry for you, friend. It's the duke's wish, 140
Whose disposition, all the world must know,
Will not be checked or stopped. I'll intercede.

KENT
Please, sir, do not. I've come far with no rest.
Some time I'll spend asleep, the rest I'll whistle.
A good man's luck can wear thin at the heels. 145
Good morning to you!

GLOUCESTER
The duke has gone too far. This won't sit well.

[Exit]

KENT
Good king, the proverb's proving to be true:
You're leaving heaven's blessing to go burn
Out in the sun! [takes out a letter] 150
Rise up, oh beacon to this globe below,
That with the comfort of your beams I may
Peruse this letter. Misery sees the light
Of miracles most. I know it's from Cordelia,
Who has quite fortunately been informed 155
Of my clandestine mission.

[strains to read in the weak light]

"...and find relief...
In monstrous times... seeking to remedy
Losses of fortune"—So weary and unrested,
Use this occasion, heavy eyes, not to
Behold my shameful lodgings. 160
Fortune, good night. Smile once more, turn your wheel!

[KENT sleeps]

Scene Three. The Open Country

[Enter EDGAR]

EDGAR
I found myself an outlaw
And in the lucky hollow of a tree
Escaped the hunt. No open port; no place
Where guards with quite uncommon vigilance
Don't lie in wait to take me. While at large,   5
I will protect myself and have a mind
To be the lowest, poorest form of beast
That poverty in its contempt for man
Could ever make. My face I'll smear with filth,
Swaddle my loins, snarl all my hair in knots,   10
And with my nakedness exposed stare down
The winds and persecutions of the sky.
This land has ample proof of beggars let from
Bedlam Asylum who with roaring voices
Stick in their numbed and bare and deadened arms   15
Pins, skewers, nails, and sprigs of rosemary;
Who, hideously displayed, from humble farms,
Poor paltry villages, sheepfolds, and mills,
Sometimes with curses, sometimes with a prayer,
Extract their charity.—Poor Tom o' Bedlam!   20
At least that's something—Edgar's nothing now.

[Exit]

Scene Four. Outside Gloucester's Castle

[Enter LEAR, FOOL, and GENTLEMAN.
KENT, disguised as Caius, is in the stocks]

LEAR
It's strange those two would just depart from home
And not send back my messenger.

GENTLEMAN
                              I've learned,

As of last night, the two had made no plans
To move from here.

KENT (masquerading as Caius)
> Hail to you, noble master!

LEAR
Ha?
Is this disgrace some joke?

KENT
> It's not my lord.

FOOL
Ha, ha! They darned those socks with heavy yarn. Horses are tied by the head, dogs and bears by the neck, monkeys by the waist, and men by the legs. If a man's too eager to test his feet, he'll get a pair of wooden stockings.

LEAR
Who could misjudge your rank so much that they
Would put you here?

KENT
> It is both he and she,
Your son-in-law and daughter.

LEAR
No.

KENT
Yes.

LEAR
No, I say.

KENT
I say, yes.

LEAR
No, no. They would not.

KENT
Yes, they have.

LEAR
By Jupiter, I swear no. 20

《KENT
By Juno, I swear yes.

LEAR》
    They would not dare.
They would not, could not do it. It's worse than murder
To do such calculating, violent outrage.
Inform me, rather quickly, as to why
You could deserve or they impose such treatment 25
On one I sent.

KENT
    My lord, when at their home
Delivering the letters from your highness,
Before I could arise from where I knelt
To show respect, in came a steaming courier.
Soaked from his haste, still panting, gasping out 30
Between his breaths some salutations from
His mistress Goneril, he gave them letters
They read at once, whose contents prompted them
To call their staff, to quickly mount their horses,
To order me to follow and to wait 35
Until they could reply—cold looks I got—
And meeting here a second messenger,
Whose welcome I perceived had poisoned mine—
Considering that he's the one who'd just
Displayed his insolence before your highness— 40
I, with more guts than sense, drew out my sword.
He roused the house with loud and fearful cries.
Your son and daughter felt this crime was worth
The shame I suffer here.

《FOOL
Winter's not yet gone if wild geese are flying south. 45

If fathers come in rags
  Their children will seem blind;
But come with money bags
  And children will be kind.
Wealth, that arrant whore, 50
Gives no keys to the poor.

So this is what your suit brings: more damages collected from your daughters than you could count in a year.»

LEAR
Oh, how this frenzy swells up toward my heart!
Hysteria's choking me—down, raging sorrow, 55
Your proper spot's below!—Where is this daughter?

KENT
Inside, sir, with the earl.

LEAR
                    Don't follow me.
Stay here.

                    [Exit]

GENTLEMAN
Was your offense no more than what you speak of?

KENT
None. 60
How come the king's here with so small a number?

FOOL
If you were put in the stocks for asking that, then you certainly deserved it.

KENT
Why, fool?

FOOL
Let's have you learn from an ant, who'll teach you not to 65 labor in winter. All those who walk behind their own noses are led by their eyes except blind men, and even then there's not one nose in twenty that cannot smell the one who's rot-

ting. Let go of a great wheel when it runs down a hill or it
will break your neck for following it; but the great one that
goes up the hill, let him drag you behind him. When a wise
man gives you better advice, then give mine back to me. I
ask no one but knaves to follow it since a fool is giving it.

> *The man who serves and looks for gain,*
> *And follows just for show,*
> *Packs up when it begins to rain,*
> *And leaves you in the snow.*
> *But I will tarry; the fool will stay,*
> *And let these smart ones run.*
> *But they're soon fools these rogues that stray;*
> *By God, this fool's not one.*

KENT
Where did you learn this, fool?

FOOL
Not in the stocks, fool.

[Re-enter LEAR, with GLOUCESTER]

LEAR
Refuse to speak with me? They're sick? They're weary?
They've traveled hard all night? Mere dodges, yes,
The sure signs of desertion and revolt.
Fetch me a better answer.

GLOUCESTER
              My lord,
You know the fiery manner of the duke,
How obstinate and fixed the man can be
To his own course.

LEAR
Vengeance! Plague! Death! Destruction!
Fiery? What "manner's" this? Why, Gloucester,
    Gloucester,
I wish to speak with Cornwall and his wife.

«GLOUCESTER
Well, my good lord, I have informed them of it.

LEAR
Informed them! Don't you understand me, man?» 95

GLOUCESTER.
Yes, my good lord.

LEAR
The King will speak with Cornwall. Her dear father
Demands his daughter's presence and her service.[4]
«Are they informed of this? My breath and blood!»
Fiery? The fiery duke? Tell the hot duke that— 100
No, not quite yet. Perhaps he is not well,
And illness will excuse us from all duties
The healthy must perform. We're not ourselves
When human nature, burdened, tells the mind
To suffer with the body. I'll back off. 105
For now I disapprove my rasher urge
To think these ailing, feverish fits could come
From a sound man. [looking toward Kent]—Death to my
   reign! Why else
Is my man here? This act persuades me
That this remoteness of the duke and her 110
Is pretence only. Turn my servant loose.
Go tell those two I wish to speak to them
Right now, at once. Tell them to come and hear me,
Or at their chamber door I'll beat a drum
Till it cries "Sleep must die." 115

GLOUCESTER
I hope it all goes well between you.

[Exit]

LEAR
O me, my pulse, my rising pulse, go down!

FOOL
Scream at it, uncle, like the squeamish cook did to the
snakes when she put 'em in a pastry still alive. She rapped
'em on their noggins with a stick and cried "Down, you 120
rascals, down!" And it was her brother who, out of pure
kindness to his horse, spread butter on its hay.

[Enter CORNWALL, REGAN,
GLOUCESTER, and SERVANTS]

LEAR
Good morning to you both.

CORNWALL
                    Hail to your grace!

[KENT is released]

REGAN
I am glad to see your highness.

LEAR
Regan, I think you are. I know the reason   125
Why I must think this, for if you were not glad,
Then I'd divorce me from your mother's tomb
For holding an adulteress. [to Kent] O, are you free?
Some other time for that. Beloved Regan,
Your sister's wicked. Regan, she has tied   130
A sharp-toothed cruelty, like a vulture, here. [points to his heart]
I dread to speak of it. You won't believe
How villainous her manner is—Oh, Regan!

REGAN
I beg you, sir, be patient. I suspect
That you neglect the value of her worth   135
Much more than she her duty.

《LEAR
                    And how is that?

REGAN
I do not think my sister in the least
Would shirk her obligation. If, sir, it's true
That she's restrained the wildness of your followers,
It's on such grounds and for such wholesome ends   140
That she's clear of all blame.》

LEAR
My curses on her!

REGAN
                    O, sir, you are old,
And nature's placed you at the very edge
Of its domain. It's best you're ruled and led
By one with judgment, who discerns your state   145
Better than you yourself. And thus, I urge you
To make your way back to our sister's home.
Say you have wronged her, sir.

LEAR
                         Ask her forgiveness?
Consider how this makes our household look.
"Dear daughter, I confess that I am old. [kneeling,   150
   mocking what he might say]
The old are useless. On my knees I beg
That you allow me clothing, bed, and food."

REGAN
Good sir, no more! These are unseemly tricks.
Return now to my sister.

LEAR
[rising]   Never, Regan.
She did away with half my entourage,   155
Looked darkly at me, striking with her tongue,
So serpent-like, into my very heart.
Let all the vengeance stored in heaven fall
On her ungrateful head! Contagious air,
Strike her unborn with lameness!

CORNWALL
                         Shame, sir, shame!   160

LEAR
O, nimble lightning, point your blinding flames
Into her scornful eyes! Infect her beauty,
You swamp-fed fogs, drawn by the powerful sun,
To fall and blister her!

REGAN
O blessèd gods! So you'll wish that on me   165
When your rash mood flares up.

LEAR
No, Regan, I will never curse you so.
Your gently-fashioned nature will not let
You turn to harshness. Her eyes are fierce, but yours
Give comfort and won't burn. I can't see you   170
Begrudging me my pleasures and my staff,
Exchanging hasty words, reducing stipends,
Or top it off by bolting up the door
To stop my coming in. You're more in tune
With duties set by nature, filial bonds,   175
Displays of courtesy, debts of gratitude,
And you did not forget that I endowed
One-half my realm to you.

REGAN
                Good sir, your point.

LEAR
Who put him in the stocks?

           [A trumpet flourish sounds]
           [Enter OSWALD]

CORNWALL
                What trumpet's that?

REGAN
My sister's. This confirms her letter's claim   180
That she would soon be here. [to Oswald] Your lady's here?

LEAR
This errand boy, whose easy, borrowed pride
Hangs on the shifting favor of his mistress.
Out of my sight, rogue.

CORNWALL
               What's all this, your grace?

LEAR
Who put my man here? Regan, I do hope   185
You did not know of it.—Who's this? O heavens!

> [Enter GONERIL]

[as if to heaven] If you esteem old men, if your kind rule
Supports obedience, if you too are old,
Make this your cause. Descend, and take my case!
[to Goneril] You're not ashamed to look upon this beard? 190

> [REGAN takes GONERIL's hand]

O Regan, is it true you'll take her hand?

GONERIL
Why not the hand, sir? How is that offensive?
Poor judgment and senescence may see harm
Where none exists.

LEAR
          O chest, you are too tough!
But can you hold? Why is he in the stocks? 195

CORNWALL
I put him there, and his misconduct, sir,
Deserved much less endorsement.

LEAR
          You did this?

REGAN
Please, father, now you're weak, so act the part.
Until the termination of your month,
You will return and live there with my sister, 200
Dismissing half your men. Then come to me.
I'm presently away from home and lack
The means required to properly receive you.

LEAR
Return to her, with fifty men dismissed?
No, better I forswear all roofs and choose 205
To fight the malice of the open air,
To be a comrade of the wolf and owl—
Necessity's sharp pinch! Return with her?
Hot-blooded France, who took without a dowry
My youngest born—I'd rather, like a squire, 210

Kneel down before his throne and beg a pension
To prop this base life up. Return with her?
Why not persuade me to be slave and packhorse
To this detested servant. [pointing to Oswald]

GONERIL
                   It's your choice, sir.

LEAR
I beg you, daughter, do not drive me mad. 215
I will not trouble you, my child. Farewell.
We'll meet no more, no longer see each other—
But you remain my flesh, my blood, my daughter,
Or rather a disease within my flesh
I'm forced to call my own. You are a boil, 220
A plague sore, you're a swollen, oozing cyst
In my infected blood. But I won't scold you.
Let shame come on its own; I won't invoke it.
I won't implore the thunder-God to shoot
Nor ask for Jove to judge you from on high. 225
Heal when you can. Get better at your leisure.
I can be patient. I can stay with Regan,
My hundred knights and I.

REGAN
                    That's not entirely so.
I'm not quite ready and cannot provide you
With a fit welcome. Listen to my sister, 230
For those who use some sense to weigh your outburst
Must then conclude that you are old, and so—
Well, she knows what she's doing.

LEAR
                    You've thought this through?

REGAN
I'd swear to it, sir. Fifty followers?
That's not enough? What could you do with more? 235
And why that many when the cost and risk
Demand a lower number? How in one home
Could such a crowd, while under two commands,
Remain at peace? It's hard, almost impossible.

GONERIL
Perhaps, my lord, you could be waited on 240
By those whom she calls servants, or by mine?

REGAN
Why not, my lord? And if their service slackens,
We could control them. If you'll just stay with me—
For now I sense there's danger—So I beg you
To bring just twenty-five. I will not house 245
And won't acknowledge more

LEAR
I gave it all to you—

REGAN
              And none too soon.

LEAR
—Made you my guardians and my trustees,
But added one condition to reserve
For me that number. What? Must I come to you 250
With five-and-twenty, Regan? Is this so?

REGAN
Don't speak of this again, my lord, with me.

LEAR
A wicked creature's face will still seem pretty
When others are more wicked; not being the worst
They earn some rank of praise.—[to Goneril] I'll go with
   you. 255
Your fifty are still double five-and-twenty,
And you pledged twice her love.

GONERIL
              Hear me, my lord.
What use are five-and-twenty, ten, or five,
To serve you in a house where twice as many
Will tend to you?

REGAN
             What need is there for one? 260

LEAR
Think not in terms of need. The meager things
Owned by the poorest beggar are superfluous.
Deny to creatures more than creatures need,
Then man's no more than beast. You are a lady.
If merely dressing warm made us look gorgeous, 265
Why, nature'd have no need for these fine things,
Which scarcely keep you warm. As for real need—
O heaven, give me that…patience, patience I need! [5]
You see me here, you gods, a poor old man,
As full of grief as age, wretched in both! 270
If it is you who stirs up daughters' hearts
Against their father, don't make me a fool
Who bears it tamely. Fill me with righteous anger,
And don't let women's weapons, water drops,
Stain this man's cheeks! No, you unnatural hags, 275
I will have such revenge upon you both
That all the world shall—I will do such things—
What they are I still can't say, but they shall be
The terrors of the earth. You think I'll weep.
No, I won't weep. 280
I have good cause for weeping, but O this heart
Will break into a hundred thousand bits
Before I'll weep. O fool, I shall go mad!

[Exit LEAR, GLOUCESTER, KENT, and FOOL]
[Storm heard at a distance]

CORNWALL
Let's go inside. A storm is coming.

REGAN
This house is small. The old man and his people 285
Cannot be lodged in comfort.

GONERIL
It's his own fault. He keeps himself from rest
So he can test his foolishness.

REGAN
If he's alone, then I'll receive him gladly,
But not one follower.

GONERIL
My intention too.
Where is my lord of Gloucester?

CORNWALL
Followed the old man out—he's just returned.

[Re-enter GLOUCESTER]

GLOUCESTER
The king is raging fiercely.

«**CORNWALL**
Where's he going?

GLOUCESTER
He wants a horse;» I don't know where he's going.

CORNWALL
Best drop the reins and let him lead himself.

GONERIL
My lord, by no means urge the man to stay.

GLOUCESTER
Good God, the night is coming; the high winds
Are stirring furiously. For miles around
There's not a bush.

REGAN
O, sir, for headstrong men
The injuries they purchase for themselves
Must be their teachers' rods. Bolt all your doors.
He is accompanied by desperate men,
And what they may incite—his ear, you know,
Invites deception—wisdom makes us fear.

CORNWALL
Bolt all your doors, my lord. It's a wild night.
My Regan counsels wisely. Out o' the storm.

[Exit]

King Lear

Act Three

Act Three

Scene One. A Heath

[A storm with thunder and lightning continues]
[Enter KENT and a GENTLEMAN, meeting]

KENT (masquerading as Caius)
Who's there, besides foul weather?

GENTLEMAN
Just one who shares the weather's agitation.

KENT
I know you. Where's the king?

GENTLEMAN
Out struggling with these fretful elements.
He tells the wind to blow the earth to sea   5
Or swell its curling waves above the land
So all might change or cease, ⟨tears his white hair,
Which these impetuous blasts, with eyeless rage,
Snatch in their fury and reduce to nothing,
Strives in his microcosm to out-storm   10
The to-and-fro-colliding wind and rain.
This night, when even cub-drained bears hole up,
And lions and the empty-bellied wolves
Keep their fur dry, he, hatless, runs and says
"Here, Fate, I wager all."⟩

KENT
                    But who is with him?   15

GENTLEMAN
None but the fool, who labors to distract him
From his heart-piercing wounds.

KENT
                            I know you, sir
And will upon the strength of what I see
Entrust to you a vital task. A rift,
Though mutual sleight-of-hand still hides its face,   20
Divides the dukes of Albany and Cornwall,
《Who—as do all whom guiding stars enthrone
And set on high—have servants, so they seem,
Who work for France as spies and keen observers
Reporting on our state. What has been seen,   25
Whether it is the plotting, squabbling dukes,
Or the hard reins the two of them have tugged
Against the kind old king, or something deeper—
And either way, these things may serve as pretexts—》
〈In any case, a force will come from France   30
Into this scattered realm; for France, already
Wise to our negligence, has planted men
In some of our best ports who wait the call
To show their arms in open. As for you,
If you will dare to place trust in my words   35
And race ahead to Dover, you will find
Some there who'll thank you for a true report
Of how unnatural, maddening sorrow gives
The king just cause to protest.
I am a gentleman of noble blood,   40
And offer with my knowledge and assurance
This duty to you.〉[1]

GENTLEMAN
First I must hear more from you.

KENT
                            No, do not.
For confirmation that there's more behind
This outer shell, look in this purse and take   45
What it contains. [hands him the purse] And should you
    see Cordelia—
And you most surely will—show her this ring,
And she will tell you who this fellow is
That you still do not know. O, curse this storm!
I'll now go seek the king.   50

GENTLEMAN
Give me your hand. Have you no more to say?

KENT
Few words, but their import outweighs the rest:
That, when we've found the king—you go that way
And I'll go this—whoever sights him first
Calls to the other. 55

[Exit in different directions]

Scene Two. Another Part of the Heath

[Storm continues]
[Enter LEAR and FOOL]

LEAR
Blow winds and burst your cheeks! Rage! Blow!
You torrents and you waterspouts, spew out
Till you've sunk steeples, drowned our weathercocks!
You sulphurous and thought-erasing fires,
You vanguards of oak-splitting thunderbolts, 5
Singe my white head! And you, all-shaking thunder,
Strike flat the pregnant roundness of the world!
Break nature's molds, spill all the seed at once
That makes ungrateful man!

FOOL
O uncle, a flood of curried favors in a dry house is better 10
than this rain water out of doors. Good uncle, go in and
ask for a blessing from your daughters. This is a night that
pities neither wise men nor fools.

LEAR
Roar till your belly's full! Spit fire! Spout rain!
Rain, wind, fire, thunder—you are not my daughters. 15
I don't charge you, you elements, with unkindness.
I've given you no kingdom nor called you children;
You owe me no allegiance, so let loose

Your horrid preference. Here I stand, your slave,
A poor, infirm, weak, and despised old man.
And yet I say that you're their servile agents
If you with these pernicious daughters throw
Your astral regiments against a head
So old and white as this! O! O! It's foul!

FOOL
He who has a house to put his head in shows he has a good one.

Find your loins a house
  Before the head has any,
You'll marry with a louse;
  In fact, you'll marry many.
The man who hurts his toe
  Just so his heart won't weep,
His corns fill him with woe
  And wake him from his sleep.

And you'll never find a pretty woman who doesn't make faces at her own reflection.

LEAR
No, I will be the mirror of all patience.
I will say nothing.

[Enter KENT]

KENT (masquerading as Caius)
Who's there?

FOOL
If truth be told, his grace and a codpiece; that is, a wise man and a fool.

KENT
Good grief, sir, you're out here? Things that love night
Don't love such nights as these. The wrathful skies
Terrify even those that prowl the dark
And keep them in their caves. I can't recall

Such sheets of fire, such bursts of horrid thunder,
Such groans of roaring wind and rain. Not since
My youth have I heard these. Man's nature cannot bear
The hardship or the fear.

LEAR
                         Let the great gods
That keep this fearsome mayhem overhead   50
Expose these culprits now. Tremble, you wretch,
Who has within yourself crimes undivulged,
Unwhipped by justice. Hide, you bloody hand,
You perjurer, you seeming man of virtue
Who is incestuous. Scoundrel, shake to pieces   55

The King and Fool in the Storm

Beneath the skilled, covert duplicity
That plots against man's life. Hushed, boxed-up crimes—
Burst open your concealing crates and beg
These vengeful judges' mercy. I am a man
More sinned against than sinning.

KENT

                            Good God, bareheaded! 60
My gracious lord, nearby here is a shed
That will afford some refuge from the tempest.
Rest here while I return to that hard house—
Much harder than the stones of which it's built,
Which even now, when I asked where you were, 65
Refused to let me in—and force them to
Restore some courtesy.

LEAR

                 My mind's begun to go.—
[to the Fool] Come on, my boy. How are you, boy? You cold?
I'm cold myself. [to Kent] Where is this straw, my fellow?
The skills necessity inspires astound 70
And make what's worthless precious.—Where's your shed?
Poor fool and knave, there's one place in my heart
That's sorry for you still.

FOOL

[singing] *He who's learned in such tiny portions*
   With hey, ho, the wind and the rain— 75
Must be content with comparable fortunes,
   For the rain it raineth every day.

LEAR
True, boy. [to Kent] Come, take us to this shed.

[Exit LEAR and KENT]

«FOOL
The night's perfect for cooling a courtesan.
I'll give a prophecy before I go: 80

When priests think it is words that matter,
When brewers thin their beer with water,
When nobles teach their tailors fashion,
No sinners burn, except from passion.
When every legal rulings right, 85
No one's in debt; not one poor knight,
When slander's never said aloud,
Pickpockets never work a crowd,
When usurers count their gold outdoors,
With churches built by pimps and whores,
It's then the realm of Albion 90
Will end in pandemonium.

Live through it all, there's one more treat,
For walking we will use our feet. ²

This is a prophecy Merlin must make, for I was born before his time.» 95

[Exit]

Scene Three. A Room in Gloucester's Castle

[Enter GLOUCESTER and EDMUND]

GLOUCESTER
God knows, Edmund, I don't like this unnatural treatment. When I sought permission to show him some mercy, they took from me the use of my own house and ordered me, at the risk of permanent disapproval, neither to speak of him, intercede for him, nor in any way care for him. 5

EDMUND
This is savage and unnatural!

GLOUCESTER
No more of that; say nothing. There's been a falling out between the dukes, and a matter more serious than that.

I received a letter this evening—it's too dangerous to read
aloud—I have locked it up. These wrongs the king is suffer- 10
ing will be avenged fully. One part of an army has already
landed. We must side with the king. I'll search for him and
secretly support him. Go and maintain a dialogue with
the duke so that my assistance won't be noticed. If he asks
for me, I am ill and gone to bed. Even if I die for it, and no 15
less is threatening me, the king, my old master, must be
helped. There are some strange things looming, Edmund.
You must be careful.

[Exit]

EDMUND
The duke must hear immediately of this
Forbidden kindness—and that letter too. 20
This seems a fair exchange and must bring me
All that my father loses—no less than all.
The younger rises when the old one falls.

[Exit]

Scene Four. A Part of the Heath with a Shed

[The storm continues]
[Enter LEAR, KENT, and FOOL]

KENT (masquerading as Caius)
Here is the place, my lord. Please, my lord, enter.
The cruelty of the open air's too rough
For humans to endure.

LEAR
    Let me alone.

KENT
Lord, enter here.

LEAR
          You want to break my heart?

KENT
I'd rather break my own. My good lord, enter.

LEAR
You think it hurts if this combative storm
Invades our skin like this. That's true for you,
But when a greater malady is present,
The lesser's barely felt. You'd flee a bear,
But if a raging sea blocked your escape,
You'd turn and face its mouth. When the mind's calm,
The body's sensitive. The tempest in my mind
Has robbed my senses of all other feeling
Except this pounding.—Filial ingratitude!
Is it as if this mouth has bit this hand
That fed it? But my vengeance will be full.
No, I will weep no more. ≪On such a night
To shut me out! Pour on. I will endure.≫
On such a night as this! O Regan, Goneril!
Your kind, old father, whose large heart gave all...
O, that way madness lies. Let me flee that!
No more of that.

KENT
          My good lord, enter here.

LEAR
Please, go on in. Look after your own needs.
This tempest won't allow me time to dwell
On things that would hurt more. But I'll go in.—
≪[to the Fool] In, boy, go first—such houseless poverty—
Yes, go on in. I'll pray, and then I'll sleep.≫

          [Exit FOOL]

Poor naked wretches, anywhere you are,
Who bear the pelting of this pitiless storm,
How will your roofless heads and unfed frames,

Your riddled, see-through raggedness, defend you
In climates such as this? To this I gave
Too little thought! Seek cures, you regal ones.
Expose yourself to feel what wretches feel
By shedding what's superfluous to them 35
And prove the skies more just.

«EDGAR
[inside the shed] We're nine feet here! We're nine feet
  deep! Poor Tom!»

[The FOOL runs out from the shed]

FOOL
Don't go in, uncle. There's a demon. Help me, help me!

KENT
Give me your hand. Who's there?

FOOL
A demon, a demon. He says his name's Poor Tom. 40

KENT
Who's doing all that mumbling in the straw?
Come out.

[Enter EDGAR, disguised as a madman]

EDGAR (masquerading as Poor Tom)
Go away! The foul fiend follows me!—[sings] "Through the
sharp hawthorn the cold wind blows."—
Hum! Go to your cold bed and warm yourself. 45

LEAR
Did you give everything to your two daughters? And then
you came to this?

EDGAR
Who gives anything to Poor Tom, whom the foul fiend
has led through fire and through flame, through ford and
whirlpool, over bog and quagmire, who has laid knives 50
under his pillow and nooses in his seat, set rat poison next
to his broth, made his heart bold enough to ride on a bay

trotting horse over four-inch-wide bridges, chasing down
his own shadow for betraying him? God protect your good
sense! Tom's a-cold.—O, do de, do de, do de. God protect   55
you from whirlwinds, ominous stars, and hexes! Give Poor
Tom some charity, whom the foul fiend torments. There I've
got him now, [slapping his body]—and there—and there
again, and there.

[The storm continues]

LEAR
Lord, have his daughters brought him to this state?—   60
Was nothing saved? You gave it all to them?

FOOL
Well, he hung onto his blanket, or we'd really be embarrassed.

LEAR
Let all impending plagues that hang above
To punish men's misdeeds land on your daughters!   65

KENT
He has no daughters, sir.

LEAR
Death, traitor! Nothing could reduce a being
To such a depth except his unkind daughters.
Is it the fashion for discarded fathers
To take so little mercy on their flesh? [indicating Edgar's   70
   condition]
Judicious punishment! It's flesh that spawned
These daughters weaned on blood.

EDGAR
Wee-wee sat on Wee-wee bluff—alow, alow, loo-loo.

FOOL
This cold night will turn us all into fools and madmen.

EDGAR
Take heed of the foul fiend. Obey your parents, keep true   75
to your word, never swear, do not commit acts with a man's
devoted spouse, do not set your sweet heart on gaudy attire.
Tom's a-cold.

LEAR
What were you before?

EDGAR
A loving servant, proud in heart and mind, who curled his   80
hair, wore his mistress's glove in his cap, satisfied the lust
in her heart, and committed the act in darkness with her,
made as many promises as he had words, and broke them
right in the sweet face of heaven; who in his dreams con-
cocted lustful schemes and awoke to do them. Wine I loved   85
deeply, dice dearly, and as for women out-haremed a sultan.
False-hearted, all ears, bloody-handed: a hog in sloth, a fox
in stealth, a wolf in greediness, a dog in madness, a lion
in preying. Don't let the creaking shoes or rustling silks
of a woman ensnare your poor heart. Keep your foot out of   90
brothels, your hand out of petticoat pleats, your name out
of lender's books, and defy the foul fiend. [sings or chants]
Through the hawthorn the cold wind still blows, saying
zoom, moom, hey no nonny. [as if keeping a dog from bolt-
ing] Dauphin, my boy, good boy, stay! Let him trot on by.[3]   95

[Storm continues]

LEAR
Why, you'd be better off in your grave than to face with
your uncovered body the ferocity of these skies. Is man no
more than this? Consider him well.—You owe the worm no
silk, the beast no leather, the sheep no wool, the whale no
perfume. Ha! The three of us this basic? You are the thing   100
itself: unequipped man is no more than a poor, bare fork of
an animal as you are. Off, off, you borrowed things! Come,
undress me now.

[LEAR tears off his own clothes]

FOOL
Please, uncle, calm yourself. It's a nasty night for a swim. You see, a tiny fire in a barren field would be like an old lecher's heart—one small spark, but the rest of his body's cold.

    [Enter GLOUCESTER with a torch]

Look, here comes a walking fire.

EDGAR
This is the foul fiend Flibbertigibbet. He begins at curfew and walks till midnight. He dims, blurs, and squints your eyes, and causes the harelip, mildews ripened wheat, and hurts the poor creatures of the earth.

> *Three times St. Withold walked the moor*
> *He met the banshee and her four;*
>   *Made her descend*
>   *And pledge to mend*
> *Her ways, so witch, away!*

KENT
How's your grace faring?

LEAR
Who's he?

KENT
Who's there? What is it you want?

GLOUCESTER
Who's there? What are your names?

EDGAR
Poor Tom, who eats the swimming frog, the toad, the tadpole, the wall-newt, and the salamander, who, in the fury of his heart, when the foul fiend rages, eats cow-dung for his salad, dines on the old rat and the dog carcass, drinks the green coating on standing pools, who is whipped from parish to parish, and punished in the stocks and imprisoned, a servant once allotted three suits for his back, six shirts for his body,

> *Horse to ride, and weapons to wear—*
> *But mice and rats and very small deer,* 130
> *Have been Tom's food for seven long year.*

Beware of my pursuer. Silence, changeling! Silence, you fiend!

GLOUCESTER
What, can't your grace find better company?

EDGAR
The prince of darkness is a gentleman: Captain Modo he's 135
called, and Captain Mahu.

GLOUCESTER
Our flesh and blood, my lord, has grown so vile
That it now hates what spawned it.

EDGAR
Poor Tom's a-cold.

GLOUCESTER
Come back with me. My loyalty to you 140
Won't yield to all your daughters' harsh commands.
Though their injunction is to bar my doors
And let this vicious darkness bring you down,
Still I have ventured all to search for you
And take you where both fire and food are ready. 145

LEAR
First let me talk some with this scientist.
What is the cause of thunder?

KENT
My good lord, take his offer. Go into the house.

LEAR
I'll have a word first with this learnèd scholar.
What do you study? 150

EDGAR
How to ward off the fiend and to kill vermin.

LEAR
Let me ask you one word in private.

KENT
Appeal to him once more to go, my lord.
His mind's begun to fragment.

GLOUCESTER
                    Can you blame him?
His daughters seek his death. Ah, that good Kent!   155
He said it would be so, poor banished man!
You say the king grows mad; I'll tell you, friend,
I am almost mad myself. I had a son,
Disowned now and condemned. He sought my death
Just now, quite recently. I loved him, friend—   160
No father's son is dearer. Truth be told,
My mind is crazed with grief. O, what a night!
I strongly urge your grace—

LEAR
                    I beg your pardon, sir.—
Noble philosopher, your company.

EDGAR
Tom's a-cold.   165

GLOUCESTER
In, fellow, there, into the shed. Keep warm.

LEAR
Let's all go in.

KENT
        This way, my lord.

LEAR
                    With him.
I won't be kept from my philosopher.

KENT
Please humor him, lord. Let him bring the fellow.

GLOUCESTER
Bring him along. 170

KENT
Let's go, fellow. Come along with us.

LEAR
Come, wise man of Athens.

GLOUCESTER
No words, no words. Hush.

EDGAR
To the dark tower young Roland came,
His motto always—Fie, foh, fum, 175
I smell the blood of an Englishman.

[Exit]

Scene Five. A Room in Gloucester's Castle

[Enter CORNWALL and EDMUND]

CORNWALL
I will have my revenge before I leave his house.

EDMUND
How I will be judged frightens me, my lord, if natural ties give way to loyalty to the state.

CORNWALL
I now realize it was not altogether your brother's evil disposition that made him seek his father's death but rather 5 just provocation, which prompted Edgar's own reprehensible badness to show itself.[4]

EDMUND
How malicious is my lot if I must repent for being righteous! This is the letter he spoke of, which proves he's providing

intelligence to France. O heavens! If this treason hadn't happened or I weren't its detector!

CORNWALL
Go with me to the duchess.

EDMUND
If the contents of this paper are correct, you have a weighty business on your hands.

CORNWALL
True or false, it has made you Earl of Gloucester. Find out where your father is so we can arrest him without trouble.

EDMUND
[aside] If I find him giving aid to the king, it will stuff him full of even more suspicion. [to Cornwall] I will continue on the side of loyalty, though the conflict between it and the ties of blood is severe.

CORNWALL
I will put my trust in you, and you will find a dearer father in my love.

[Exit]

Scene Six. In a Farmhouse Near the Castle

[Enter GLOUCESTER, LEAR, KENT, FOOL, and EDGAR]

GLOUCESTER
This is better than the open air. Take it thankfully. I will augment the comfort it offers in any way I can. I will not be gone long.

KENT (masquerading as Caius)
All his mental powers have given way to his rage. The gods
reward your kindness! 5

[Exit GLOUCESTER]

EDGAR (masquerading as Poor Tom)
The devil Frateretto calls me and tells me Emperor Nero
is an angler in the lake of darkness.—[to the Fool] Pray,
simpleton, and beware the foul fiend.

FOOL
Please tell me, uncle, whether a madman is a gentleman
or a commoner. 10

LEAR
A king, a king!

«FOOL
No, he's a commoner who has a gentleman as a son, for he
goes mad when he sees his son become a gentleman before
he does.

LEAR»
To have a thousand with red burning skewers 15
Go hissing into them—

‹EDGAR
The foul fiend bites my back. [removes a flea].

FOOL
You're mad if you trust the tameness of a wolf, a horse's
health, a boy's love, or a whore's word.

LEAR
It shall be done. They shall stand trial at once.— 20
[to Edgar] Come, sit down here, most learnèd of all
    judges.
[to the Fool] You, sapient sir, sit here. Now you she-foxes!

EDGAR
Look, where he stands and glares! Do you need spectators

at your trial, madam? [sings] "Come over the brook, Bessy, to me,"—

FOOL
Her hull is now leaking,
So she is not speaking
Of why she dares not come over to thee.

EDGAR
The foul fiend haunts poor Tom in the voice of a nightingale. The demon Hoppedance cries in Tom's belly for two white herring. No, you growling, dark angel. I have no food for you.

KENT
How are you, sir? Don't stand there dumbfounded.
Will you lie down and rest upon these cushions?

LEAR
I'll watch their trial first. Bring in the evidence.
[to Edgar, wearing a blanket] You, robe-clad man of justice, take your place.
[to the Fool] And you, his partner in all matters legal,
Sit by his side. [to Kent] You too are on the bench.
You join them there.

EDGAR
Let us be just. [sings]
Are you sleeping or waking, you jolly shepherd?
    Your sheep are in the corn.
With only one blast from your delicate mouth
    Your sheep will do no harm.
Purr, the demon cat is gray.

LEAR
Arraign her first. This is Goneril. [indicating a stool] I hereby swear under oath before this honorable assembly: she kicked the poor king her father.

FOOL
Come forward, mistress. Is your name Goneril?

LEAR
She cannot deny it.

FOOL
Pardon me, I thought you were a stool. 50

LEAR
And here's another, whose warped looks reveal
What stuff her heart is made of. Stop her there!
Arms, arms! Sword! Fire!—There's bribery in the court!
False justices, why have you let her flee?>

EDGAR
Heaven protect your sanity! 55

KENT
O pity! Sir, where is that self-control
That you so often claim to have retained?

EDGAR
[aside] I'm now so taken with his plight my tears
Will ruin my deception.

LEAR
The little dogs and all, 60
Tray, Blanch, and Sweetheart, see, they bark at me.

EDGAR
Tom will shake his head at them.—Away, you curs!

No matter whether black or white
The tooth is poison should it bite.
Mastiff, greyhound, mongrel brutal, 65
Hound or spaniel, bitch or poodle,
If bobtailed pup or drooping tail—
Tom will make them weep and wail;
For when I turn and shake my head,
Dogs leap the gate and run in dread. 70

Do de, de, de. Shoo! Come, march to festivals and fairs and
market-towns. Poor Tom, your cup is dry.

LEAR
Then let them dissect Regan. See what's built up in her heart. Is there a natural cause that makes these hearts so hard?—[to Edgar] You, sir, I invite you to be one of my hundred. Only I do not like the style of your garments. You'll say they're exotic, but let them be changed.

KENT
Now, my good lord, lie here and rest awhile.

LEAR
Make no noise, make no noise. Draw the curtains. Good, good. We'll go to supper in the morning.

«**FOOL**
And I'll go to bed at noon.»

[Re-enter GLOUCESTER]

GLOUCESTER
Come here, my friend. Where is the king, my master?

KENT
Here, sir, but don't disturb him—he's lost his mind.

GLOUCESTER
Friend, if you would, please take him in your arms.
I overheard a plot of death against him.
There is a litter ready; lay him in it
And drive towards Dover, friend, where you will be
Both welcomed and protected. Lift up your master.
If you delay for half an hour, his life
And yours and all who offer to defend him
Are risking certain loss. Lift up, lift up,
And follow me to where we can obtain
Some quick provisions.

‹**KENT**
              Overwhelmed, we sleep.
This rest perhaps will soothe your injured nerves,
Which will, unless these circumstances change,
Resist a cure.—[to the Fool] Come, help us with your

master.
You must not stay behind.

GLOUCESTER⟩
                    Come, come, away!

   [Exit KENT, GLOUCESTER, and FOOL,
               carrying LEAR]

⟨**EDGAR**
When we see that our betters share our woes,
No longer do our miseries seem foes.
Alone we suffer mostly in our mind   100
And leave our carefree, happy sights behind.
But so much of our suffering we don't see,
When grief has mates, and pain has company.
How light and portable now is my pain,
While that which makes me bend makes our king strain.   105
His children and my father!—Tom, you go!
Take note of talk and let your true self show
When all these claims that make you so deplored
Prove to be false and honor is restored.
Tonight whatever happens, save the king!   110
Hide, hide.⟩

                    [Exit]

Scene Seven. A Room in Gloucester's Castle

       [Enter CORNWALL, REGAN, GONERIL,
              EDMUND, and SERVANTS]

CORNWALL
[to Goneril] Ride swiftly to my lord your husband. Show
him this letter. The army of France has landed. Search for
the traitor Gloucester.

             [Exit some of the SERVANTS]

REGAN
Hang him instantly.

GONERIL
Pluck out his eyes.

CORNWALL
Leave him to endure my displeasure.—Edmund, keep my sister-in-law company. The revenge we are bound to take upon your traitorous father is not fit for you to witness. Go to the duke and advise him to mobilize at once. We are forced to do the same. Our riders will quickly relay intelligence between us. Farewell, dear sister. [to Edmund] Farewell, my lord of Gloucester.

[Enter OSWALD]

Ah, yes! Where's the king?

OSWALD
My lord of Gloucester's bringing him here now.
Some thirty-six or -seven of Lear's knights,
In hot pursuit, met Gloucester on the way,
Who, joining up with more of his attendants,
Have gone with him towards Dover, where they boast
Of having well-armed friends.

CORNWALL
Get horses for your mistress.

GONERIL
Farewell, sweet lord, and sister.

CORNWALL
Edmund, farewell.

[Exit GONERIL, EDMUND, and OSWALD]

Go find the traitor Gloucester,
Shackle him like a thief, bring him before us.

[Exit other SERVANTS]

It's hardly proper to condemn the man
Without some form of hearing, yet our power 25
Allows our wrath some latitude, which men
May fault but won't restrain.

[Re-enter servants, with GLOUCESTER]

Who's there? The traitor?

REGAN
Ungrateful fox! It's him.

CORNWALL
Bind tight his shriveled arms.

GLOUCESTER
Your graces, what's all this? Good friends, remember 30
You are my guests here. Stop this foul play, friends.

CORNWALL
Bind him, I say.

[SERVANTS bind him]

REGAN
Tight, tight.—O filthy traitor!

GLOUCESTER
Unmerciful lady, you are one, not me.

CORNWALL
To this chair bind him.—Villain, you will find—

[REGAN plucks his beard]

GLOUCESTER
By the kind gods, this scoffs at all that's noble 35
To pluck me by the beard.

REGAN
So white, and such a traitor!

GLOUCESTER
                    Wicked lady,
These hairs which you have stolen from my chin
Will rise up and accuse you. I'm your host.
The face of hospitality should not   40
Be scuffed by robbers' hands. What do you want?

CORNWALL
What messages have you received from France?

REGAN
Straight-forward answers, for we know the truth.

CORNWALL
And what alliance joins you with these traitors
Who've landed in the kingdom?   45

REGAN
In whose hands have you placed the lunatic king? Speak!

GLOUCESTER
I have a letter—it's conjecture mostly—
Which comes from one who has a neutral heart,
And not from one opposed.

CORNWALL
                    Cunning.

REGAN
                              And false.

CORNWALL
Where have you sent the king?   50

GLOUCESTER
To Dover.

REGAN
Why Dover? Didn't that endanger you—

CORNWALL
But why to Dover? Let him first answer that.

GLOUCESTER
Cornered by dogs, I must endure their teeth.

REGAN
But why to Dover, sir?   55

GLOUCESTER
Because I will not watch your savage nails
Pluck out his poor old eyes or your cruel sister
Stick boarish fangs into his hallowed flesh.
Though such a sea, whose storm his naked head
Endured in hell-black night, could have bobbed up   60
And doused the stellar fires,
Yet, poor old man, he helped the heavens rain.
If wolves outside had howled at that dire time,
You'd have to say, "Good doorman, let them in."
Even the cruel do that[5]...but I will see   65
The wings of holy vengeance catch such children.

CORNWALL
You'll never see it.—Fellows, hold the chair.
Upon these eyes of yours I'll place my foot.

   [GLOUCESTER is held down in his chair, while CORN-
       WALL digs out an eye and stamps on it]

GLOUCESTER
Whoever hopes to live till he is old,
Give me some help!—O savage!—O you gods!   70

REGAN
One side will mock the other. Do it too!

CORNWALL
If you see vengeance—

FIRST SERVANT
                Go no further, sir.

I've served you ever since I was a child,
But never could I serve you better than
To ask you now to halt.

REGAN
      What's this, you dog?   75

FIRST SERVANT
If you were wearing whiskers on your chin,
I'd shake you by them. What's the point of this?

CORNWALL
My servant?
    [Draws and runs at him]

FIRST SERVANT
Well, then, come on, and risk what anger brings.

  [Draws. They fight. CORNWALL is wounded]

REGAN
[to another servant] Give me your sword—A serf resists
 like this?   80

 [Snatches a sword, comes from behind, and stabs him]

FIRST SERVANT
O, I am dying!—My lord, there's still one eye
To see that harm comes to him. O!

       [Dies]

CORNWALL
One eye to see? Take this, then. Out, vile jelly!

   [Digs out GLOUCESTER's other eye
    and throws it on the ground]

Where is your luster now?

GLOUCESTER
All dark and none to help! Where's my son Edmund?   85
Edmund, make all the sparks of natural bonds
Avenge this horrid act.

REGAN
                    Out, treacherous villain!
You call for one who hates you. It was he
Who first disclosed your acts of treason to us,
One who's too good to pity you.   90

GLOUCESTER
O my follies! Then Edgar has been wronged.
Kind gods, forgive my part and help him thrive!

REGAN
Go shove him out the gate and let him smell
His way to Dover. And you, my lord? How are you?

CORNWALL
I have received a wound. Follow me, lady.—   95
Toss out that eyeless villain. Throw this slave
Upon the dung heap.—Regan, I'm bleeding freely.
Bad timing for a wound. Give me your arm.

        [Exit CORNWALL, led by REGAN]
   [SERVANTS untie GLOUCESTER and lead him out]

⟨**SECOND SERVANT**
I'll never need to fear my wickedness
If this man's end is good.

THIRD SERVANT
                    If she lives long,   100
And in the end she meets a natural death,
All women will be monsters.

SECOND SERVANT
Let's follow the old earl and get the madman
To be his guide. These roaming lunatics
Can wander where they wish.   105

THIRD SERVANT
You go. I'll fetch some cotton and a salve
To treat his bleeding face. Now heaven help him!

           [Exit in different directions]⟩

King Lear

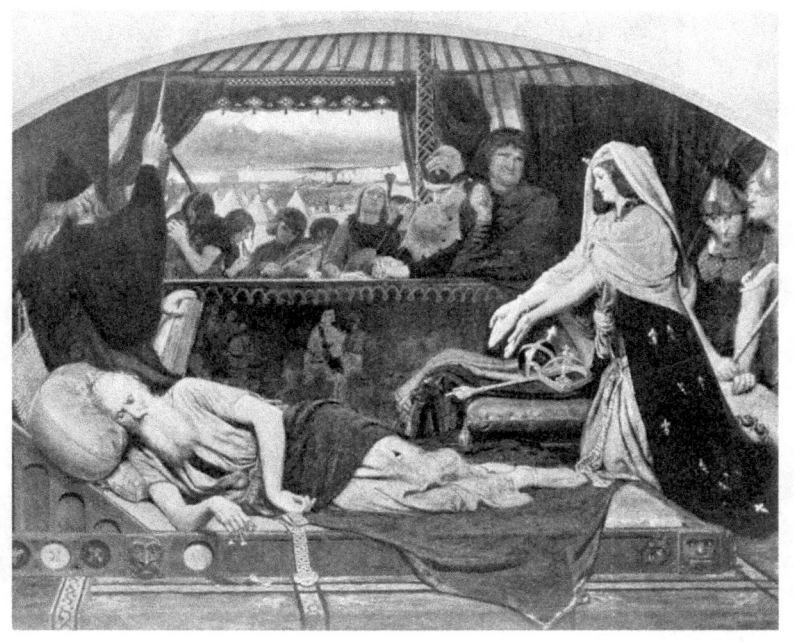

Act Four

Act Four

Scene One. The Heath

[Enter Edgar]

EDGAR (as Poor Tom)
Better like this, to know that one's despised,
Than still despised and flattered. For the worst,
The lowest thing, the most cast down by fortune,
Is always hopeful, never fearing loss.
The change we most lament is from the best; 5
The worst returns to laughter. «Welcome, then,
You insubstantial air that I embrace!
This wretch to whom your winds have blown their worst
Owes nothing to your blasts.»

[Enter GLOUCESTER, led by an OLD MAN]

—But who is this?
My father, bloody-eyed?[1]—World, world, O world! 10
If strange reversals didn't make us hate you,
Life would not yield to death.

OLD MAN (tenant to Gloucester)
O my good lord,
I've been your tenant and your father's tenant
For eighty years.

GLOUCESTER
Away, you get away. Good friend, be gone. 15
Your kindness will do me no good at all;
And it may harm you.

OLD MAN
You cannot see the path.

GLOUCESTER
I have no path and therefore need no eyes.
I stumbled when I saw. It's seen so often:
Wealth makes us careless and our deprivations   20
Turn out to be our assets. O dear Edgar,
The fuel that fed your hoodwinked father's wrath!
Were I to live to see you with my touch,
I'd say that I had eyes again!

OLD MAN
                    [sees Edgar] Who's there?

EDGAR.
[aside] O gods! How could I say "I'm at my worst?"   25
When now I'm worse than ever.

OLD MAN
                    It's poor mad Tom.

EDGAR
[aside] I may be worse off yet. It's not the worst
As long as we can say "This is the worst."

OLD MAN
Friend, where're you going?

GLOUCESTER
                    Is it a beggar-man?

OLD MAN
Madman and beggar too.   30

GLOUCESTER
He has some reasoning, or he could not beg.
In last night's storm I saw a man like this,
Which made me think a man's a worm. My son
Then came into my mind, and yet my mind
Was scarcely friends with him. I've heard more since.   35
As flies to thoughtless boys are we to gods—
They kill us just for sport.

EDGAR
[aside]   How could this be?—

Bad course I'm on, to play the fool to sorrow
And irk myself and others. [to Gloucester] Bless you,
    master!

GLOUCESTER
Is that the naked fellow?

OLD MAN
                    Yes, my lord.   40

GLOUCESTER
I ask you then to leave us. For my sake
Catch up to us a mile or two ahead,
Toward Dover. Do it out of ancient love,
And bring some clothing for this naked soul,
Whom I'll entreat to lead me.

OLD MAN
                    But, sir, he's mad.   45

GLOUCESTER
Sick times these are when madmen lead the blind.
Do what I ask, or rather what you wish.
Above all, please be gone.

OLD MAN
I'll bring the best apparel that I have,
Whatever comes of that.

                    [Exit]

GLOUCESTER
                    You, naked fellow—   50

EDGAR
Poor Tom's a-cold. [aside] This act is wearing thin.

GLOUCESTER
Come here, my fellow.

EDGAR
[aside] And yet I must.—[to Gloucester] Bless your sweet
    eyes, they bleed.

GLOUCESTER
You know the way to Dover?

EDGAR
Each fence and gate on horse trail or footpath. Poor Tom's 55
been scared out of his blessed wits. The gods protect you,
good man's son, from the foul fiend! ⟨Five fiends have been
inside poor Tom at once: the lord of lust, Obidicut; Hobbidi-
dence, prince of muteness; Mahu, stealing; Modo, murder;
Flibbertigibbet, smirking and grimacing—who've since left 60
to possess chambermaids and ladies-in-waiting. So, may
the gods protect you, master!⟩

GLOUCESTER
Here, take this [hands him his coin purse], you whom
   every plague of heaven
Has humbled with each blow. What makes me wretched
Will make you happier. Heavens, do this always! 65
Let the extravagant and lust-fed man,
Who makes your laws serve him, who will not see
Because he does not feel, feel your power soon!
Then distribution will undo excess,
And all will have enough. Do you know Dover? 70

EDGAR
Yes, master.

GLOUCESTER
There is a cliff, whose high and arching head
Looks grimly down upon the deep below.
Just bring me to the very brim of it,
And I'll repair the misery you now bear 75
With something precious with me. Once I'm there,
I will not need a guide.

EDGAR
                 Give me your arm.
Poor Tom will guide you.

                [Exit]

Scene Two. Outside the Duke of Albany's Palace

[Enter GONERIL and EDMUND]

GONERIL
It's odd, my lord, that on our way we did
Not meet my timid husband.

[Enter OSWALD]

Where's your master?

OSWALD
Inside, but never was a man so changed.
I told him of the army that has landed;
He smiled at that. I told him you were coming;
His answer was, "The worst." Of Gloucester's treachery   5
And of the loyal service of his son,
When I informed him, he called me a fool

And told me I had things all turned around.
What he should most dislike seems pleasing to him;
What pleased him, now offends.

GONERIL
[to Edmund]   Then go no further.   10
It is the cowering terror of his spirit
That dares him not to act. He looks past wrongs
That need reprisal. Our hopes expressed while traveling
May be fulfilled. Go, Edmund, back to Cornwall.
Speed up enlistments there and lead his troops.   15
I must switch roles at home and put the knitting
Into my husband's hands. This trusty servant
Will relay news, so soon you'll likely hear,
If you will dare to think of your own needs,
A mistress's command. [giving a favor] Wear this; don't
    speak;   20
Lower your head. This kiss, if it has worked,
Should raise your spirit up into the air.
Plant these seeds deep, and fare thee well.

EDMUND
Yours even if they're spent.

[Exit]

GONERIL
                My dearest Gloucester.
«O, the difference from man to man!»   25
To you a woman's services are owed;
A fool usurps my bed.²

OSWALD
            Madam, here comes my lord.

[Exit]
[Enter ALBANY]

GONERIL
I guess I'm worth a whistle.

ALBANY
                    Goneril,
You are not worth the dust which the rude wind
Blows in your face! ⟨Your nature frightens me.   30
A creature that disdains its origin
Cannot be kept within its boundaries.
She who will lop off and debranch herself
From her essential sap will no doubt wither
And join the woodpile.   35

GONERIL
No more. This sermon's foolish.

ALBANY
Wisdom and goodness to the vile seem vile.
Filth savors only filth. What have you done?
Tigers, not daughters, what have you achieved?
A father, and a kindly, agèd man,   40
Revered so much a caged-up bear would lick him,
So barbarously, perversely driven mad.
Could my dear brother-in-law let you do it?
A man, a prince, who gained so much from him!
And if embodied spirits sent from heaven   45
Don't fall at once to tame these vile offenders,
Then surely it will come:
Humanity will prey upon itself,
Like monsters of the deep.⟩

GONERIL
                    You spineless man,
Who turns his cheek, whose head invites abuse;   50
Who lacks beneath his brow an eye to tell him
When to stand firm or yield; ⟨who doesn't know
That only fools neglect to punish villains
Before they do their mischief. Where's your drum?
France spreads his banners in our quiet land,   55
With feathered helmets, threatening your state,
While you, high-minded fool, sit still and cry
"Gosh, why's he doing this?"⟩

ALBANY
                    Look closely, devil!
Deformity, expected in a fiend,
Looks even ghastlier in you.

GONERIL
                    Vain fool!   60

⟨**ALBANY**
You changed and self-concealing, shameless thing!
Don't let the monster show. If only I
Could let these hands obey my inclination.
Ready they are to wrench apart and tear
Your flesh and bones. However much a fiend,   65
A woman's shape still shields you.

GONERIL
Meow, your manhood's slipped its cage.⟩³

            [Enter a MESSENGER]

⟨**ALBANY**
What news?⟩

MESSENGER
O, my good lord, the Duke of Cornwall's dead,
Slain by his servant, trying to put out   70
The other eye of Gloucester.

ALBANY
                    Gloucester's eyes?

MESSENGER
A servant that he reared, pierced by compassion,
Stepped in to stop the deed, pointing his sword
At his great master, who, enraged by this,
Flew at the servants, stabbing him to death,   75
But not without one harmful wound which since
Has plucked the life from him.

ALBANY
                        You're still above,
Heavenly judge, so earthly crimes like these
Can quickly be avenged!—But, O poor Gloucester!
Has he lost both his eyes?

MESSENGER
                     Both, both, my lord.—   80
This letter, madam, needs a speedy answer.
It's from your sister.

GONERIL
                [aside] In one way I am glad.
But being widowed, and my Gloucester with her,
Might gouge away the groundwork of my dreams
And leave a hate-filled life. In other ways   85
The news is not so sour. [aloud] I'll read, then answer.

                [Exit]

ALBANY
Where was his son when they put out his eyes?

MESSENGER
Here with my lady.

ALBANY
          But he's not here now.

MESSENGER
No, my good lord. I saw him going back.

ALBANY
Is he part of this wickedness?   90

MESSENGER
Yes, my lord. He informed against the earl
And left the house on purpose, so their punishment
Could run a freer course.

ALBANY
                    Gloucester, I live
To thank you for the love you've showed the king
And to avenge your eyes.—Come with me friend.   95
Tell me what else you know.

                    [Exit]

⟨**Scene Three. The French Camp near Dover**

[Enter KENT (as Caius) and a GENTLEMAN]

KENT
Why has the king of France gone back so suddenly? Do you know the reason?

GENTLEMAN
Something left unresolved in his country, which since his coming here has surfaced and which portends for his kingdom so much fear and danger that his personal return was   5
indeed required and necessary.

KENT
Who has he left behind to lead his men?

GENTLEMAN
The Marshal of all France, Monsieur La Far.

KENT
Did your letters prod the queen to any demonstration of grief?   10

GENTLEMAN
Yes, sir, she took them, read them in my presence,
And now and then an ample tear rolled down
Her lovely cheek. She seemed to be a queen
Of her emotions, which, quite rebel-like,
Had sought to be her king.

KENT
                    O, then it moved her.   15

GENTLEMAN
Not to a rage. Restraint and sorrow strove
To best express her beauty. You have seen
The sun shine through the rain. Her smiles and tears
Were that, but more. That happy bit of smile
That played on her ripe lips seemed not to know 20
What guests were in her eyes, which fell from there
As pearls might drop from diamonds.—In short, sorrow
Would be a fine thing much adored if it
Were always so becoming.

KENT
                    She said nothing?

GENTLEMAN
She panted once or twice in heaving breaths 25
Her father's name, as if it pressed her heart.
Cried "Sisters, sisters!—Shameless ladies! Sisters!
Kent! Father! Sisters! What, the storm? At night?
Who now believes in pity?"—Then she shook
The holy water from her heavenly eyes. 30
Her anguish moistened, she then broke away
To deal with grief alone.

KENT
                    It is the stars.
The stars above must rule our dispositions,
Or else one's self and mate could not beget
Such different offspring. Have you two spoken since? 35

GENTLEMAN
No.

KENT
Before the king of France went back?

GENTLEMAN
                    No, since.

KENT
Well, sir, the poor, afflicted Lear's in town here,
And sometimes when he's more in tune recalls

What brought this on and won't by any means   40
Consent to see his daughter.

GENTLEMAN
                    Why, good sir?

KENT
A shame too powerful jostles him. His cruelty,
Which stripped her of his blessing, turned her out
To foreign perils, and gave her precious claims
To his dog-hearted daughters—these things sting   45
His mind so full of venom that burning shame
Won't let him near Cordelia.

GENTLEMAN
                    The poor man.

KENT
No word on Albany's and Cornwall's forces?

GENTLEMAN.
There is. They're on the march.

KENT
Well, sir, I'll take you to our master Lear   50
Where you can tend to him. Important business
Will keep me in concealment for a time.
When I'm myself again, you won't regret
Extending your acquaintance. Please, sir, come
Along with me.   55

                    [Exit]>

Scene Four. A Tent in the French Camp

    [Enter CORDELIA, PHYSICIAN, and SOLDIERS]

CORDELIA
Alas, it's he. Yes, just now he was seen,
As mad as a vexed sea, singing aloud,

Crowned with sharp nettles and rank, bitter weeds,
With thistles, hemlock, ragweed, cuckoo-flowers,
Crabgrass, and all the useless weeds that grow 5
In our sustaining fields. Send out a hundred.
Search every acre in the high-grown fields,
And place him in our care. [exit an Officer] What can our science
Do to restore to him his stolen mind?
My worldly goods go to the one who helps him. 10

Physician (serving Cordelia and Lear)
There are ways, madam.
The foster nurse of nature is good rest,
And that he lacks, and to induce that state
There are effective herbs that have the power
To close the eye to pain.

CORDELIA
                    All secret blessings, 15
All the unpublished powers of the earth,
Sprout with my tears! Deliver aid and remedy
To the good man's distress! Search, search for him,
Or untamed frenzy will undo a life
That lacks the means to lead itself.

            [Enter a MESSENGER]

MESSENGER
                    News, madam. 20
The British force is marching toward us now.

CORDELIA
We were forewarned. Our troops are battle-ready
In expectation of them. O dear father,
It is your house that I must be in now.
It seems my grief 25
And pleading tears have earned great France's pity.
Puffed up ambitions don't prod us to fight,
But love, dear love, and our old father's right.
Soon may I see and hear him!

                [Exit]

Scene Five. A Room in Gloucester's Castle

[Enter REGAN and OSWALD]

REGAN
Has Albany dispatched his force?

OSWALD
                           Yes, madam.

REGAN
Is he there with them?

OSWALD
               After much ado.
Your sister is the better soldier.

REGAN
You're sure Lord Edmund never spoke with him?

OSWALD
No, madam. 5

REGAN
What could my sister's letter to him say?

OSWALD
I don't know, lady.

REGAN
He must have rushed off on a serious matter.
A major blunder, Gloucester's eyes put out
Yet left alive. Now anywhere he goes 10
Hearts turn against us. Edmund, I think, has left,
Concerned about his suffering, to dispatch
His night-filled life as well as to observe
The power of our enemy.

OSWALD
I must go after him, madam, with my letter. 15

REGAN
Our troops will march tomorrow. Stay with us.
The roads are dangerous.

OSWALD
                    I cannot, madam.
My lady's orders to me were precise.

REGAN
Why write to Edmund? Couldn't you convey
Her message verbally? Most likely, it's—
I don't know what it is. I'd be quite pleased,
If I could see the letter.

OSWALD
                    Madam, I'd rather —

REGAN
I know your lady does not love her husband.
I'm sure of that. The last time she was here,
She made strange eyes and sent quite telling looks
Towards noble Edmund. I know you're in her trust.

OSWALD
I, madam?

REGAN
I'm certain that it's true. You are. I know it.
So I advise you to take note of this:
My lord is dead. Edmund and I have talked.
It is more fitting that he take my hand
And not your lady's. You can guess the rest.
If you do find him, you must give him this, [hands a
    letter or token]
And when your lady hears all this from you,
I hope she calls good sense back to her side.
So, fare you well.
If by some chance you hear of that blind traitor,
Promotion comes to him who cuts him down.

OSWALD
If I could meet him, madam, I would show
Which faction I am following.

REGAN
             Farewell.   40

             [Exit]

Scene Six. The Country Near Dover

    [Enter EDGAR, dressed as a peasant, and
          GLOUCESTER]

GLOUCESTER
You said you'd take me to a cliff. But when?

EDGAR
You're climbing towards it now. See? We're struggling.

GLOUCESTER
The ground seems level.

EDGAR
             It is horribly steep.
Wait, can you hear the sea?

GLOUCESTER
             No, not at all.

EDGAR
Your other senses then are growing weak   5
From your eyes' agony.

GLOUCESTER
             It may well be.
It seems your speech has changed, with choice of phrase
And reasoning much better than before.

EDGAR
You're much deceived. In no way have I changed,
Except my garments.

GLOUCESTER
          Your speech seems more refined.

EDGAR
Come on, sir. Here's the place. Stand still. How fearful
And dizzying to cast one's eyes down there.
The crows and gulls that flap the air midway
Appear as small as beetles. Half way down
An herb collector hangs. A frightening job!
He seems to be no bigger than his head.
The fishermen that walk upon the beach
Look just like mice, and those tall ships at anchor
Are life boats now and their life boats are buoys
Almost too small to see. The murmuring surge
That chafes against the countless, useless pebbles
Cannot be heard up here.—I'll look no more,
Or else my spinning mind and whirling eyes
Will topple downward with me.

GLOUCESTER
          Stand me there.

EDGAR
Give me your hand—the edge is half a foot
Away. For all that lies beneath the moon
I would not leap straight up.

GLOUCESTER
          Release my hand.
Friend, here's another purse; in it's a jewel
Well worth a poor man's trouble. Gods and fairies
Will multiply it! Move yourself back some.
Bid me farewell, and let me hear you leaving.

EDGAR
Now fare you well, good sir. [pretends to go]

GLOUCESTER
                    That I will do.

EDGAR
[aside] The reason I must toy with his despair
Is so that I may cure it.

GLOUCESTER
                    O, mighty gods! [kneeling]
This world I now renounce, and in your sight,   35
I calmly cast my great affliction off.
If I could bear it longer and not rise
Against your great indomitable will,
The dying wick of this loathed creature would
Burn itself out. If Edgar lives, O, bless him!—   40
Farewell now, fellow.

EDGAR
                    Going, sir. Farewell.—

[GLOUCESTER leaps and falls on the ground]

And yet I worry that the mind can rob
The treasury of life when life itself
Approves the theft. If he were where he thought,
All thought would now be past. Alive or dead?   45
[as Edgar, not Poor Tom] Oh, sir! Oh, friend! Please,
    sir?—Please, speak!
Perhaps he did die. No, he's coming to.
What are you made of?

GLOUCESTER
                    Go, and let me die.

EDGAR
If you were more than gossamer, feathers, air,
(And plummeting so many fathoms down),   50
You'd splatter like an egg, but you are breathing,
Are made of flesh, no blood, can speak, seem sound.
Ten masts stacked end to end could not have reached

The altitude from which you just now fell.
To have survived's a miracle. Speak again.   55

GLOUCESTER
But did I fall, or not?

EDGAR
Down from the dreadful summit's chalky edge.
Look up above. The shrill-voiced lark's so high
It can't be seen or heard. Just look up there.

GLOUCESTER
Mercy, I have no eyes.   60
Is wretchedness denied the benefit
Of ending grief with death? There's still some comfort
If misery can cheat the tyrant's rage
And frustrate his proud will.

EDGAR
                    Give me your arm.
There. That's it. Up now. Can you use your legs?   65

GLOUCESTER
Too well, too well.

EDGAR
            This is beyond all strangeness.
Way up there on the peak, what was that thing
That parted from you?

GLOUCESTER
            A poor unfortunate beggar.

EDGAR
As I stood here below, it seemed his eyes
Were two full moons. He had a thousand noses,   70
Horns curled and twisted like the furrowed sea.
It was some fiend. So, fortunate old man,
Trust that the purest gods, who earn their reverence
By doing the impossible, have saved you.

GLOUCESTER
Yes, I recall him. From now on I'll bear   75

Affliction till it cries out to itself
"Enough!" and lets me die. I took that thing
You speak of for a man. It often said
"The fiend, the fiend"—he led me to that place.

EDGAR
Have calm and carefree thoughts.—Now who is this?

[Enter LEAR, strangely dressed up with flowers]

A saner mind would never decorate
Its owner in this way.

LEAR
No, they can't haul me in for making coins. I am the king himself.

EDGAR
O, you heart-piercing sight!

LEAR
[studying his image on a coin] Nature's superior to art in this case.[4] Here's your recruitment bonus. That fellow handles his bow like a farm boy. Give me a three-foot draw.—Look, look, a mouse! Peace now! This piece of toasted cheese will do it. There's my gauntlet [throws down his glove]; I'll challenge a giant. Bring up the pikers. O, good flight, bird!—Bull's-eye, bull's-eye. Hyooh! [imitates the sound of an arrow]—What's the password?

EDGAR
Sweet marjoram.

LEAR
Pass.

GLOUCESTER
I know that voice. [falls to his knees]

LEAR
Ha! Goneril with a white beard? They groveled before me

like dogs and told me I had wisdom's white beard even
before the black one was there. To say "yes, sir" and "no,
sir" to everything that I said "yes" and "no" to was not
sincere theology. When the rain came to soak me and the
wind to make me chatter, when the thunder would not
hush at my command, that's when I exposed 'em, that's
when I sniffed 'em out. Come now, they are not men of
their words. They told me I was everything; it's a lie—I'm
not immune to fevers.

GLOUCESTER
The tone of that voice I remember well.
Is it the king?

LEAR
              Ay, every inch a king.
When I stare down, see how my subjects quake.
I pardon this man's life.—What is the charge?—
Adultery?—
You shall not die. Die for adultery? No,
The wren goes at it; the small gilded fly
Is lecherous in my sight.
Let copulation thrive, for Gloucester's bastard son
Was kinder to his father than the daughters
Conceived between my lawful sheets.
Go at it, lust, pell-mell! For I lack soldiers.
Behold that simpering dame there,
Whose face forewarns of snow between her prongs;
Who sports her bits of virtue and shakes her head
When she hears pleasure's name.
The polecat and the feisty horse don't do it
With a more frantic appetite.
Below the waist they're centaurs,
Though women up above.
Down to the waist is what the gods possess;
The rest goes to the fiend. The hole of hell
And darkness, a sulphurous pit; burning, scalding,
Stench, decay. Damn, damn, damn! Puh, Puh!
Give me an ounce of fragrance, good apothecary.
Sweeten my imagination. Here's money for you.

GLOUCESTER
O, let me kiss that hand!

LEAR
Let me wipe it first; it smells of mortality.

GLOUCESTER
O ruined work of nature! This great world   135
Wears down like this to nothing. Do you know me?

LEAR
I remember your eyes well enough. Are you squinting at
me? No, do your worst, blind Cupid; I don't want love. Read
this challenge. Note only the handwriting.

GLOUCESTER
Were all its letters suns, I'd still not see them.   140

EDGAR
[aside] Heard second-hand, I'd swear this wasn't true.
It's true and breaks my heart.

LEAR
Read.

GLOUCESTER
What, with these holes for eyes?

LEAR
Aha, is that what you mean? No eyes in your head, nor   145
money in your purse? Your eyes are in a deep, dark hole,
your purse is light, yet you see how this world works.

GLOUCESTER
I see by feeling.

LEAR
What, are you mad? A man can see how the world works
without eyes. Look with your ears. See how that judge over 150
there reprimands that common thief. Hear it with your ears.
Switch places, and which hand is it in? [mimes sleight of

hand] Which is the judge, which is the thief? Have you seen a farmer's dog bark at a beggar?

GLOUCESTER
Yes, sir.

LEAR
And the creature run from the cur? There you can behold a mighty symbol of authority: an office obeyed that's held by a dog.
You rascal flogger, restrain your bloody hand!
Why do you whip that whore? Bare your own back.
You hotly lust to use her for an act
For which you whip her. The usurer hangs the cheat.
Through tattered clothes small vices show so clear.
Robes and fur coats hide all. «Coat sin with gold,
And the strong lance of justice gently breaks.
Shield it with rags, a piece of straw will pierce it.
None guilty—I say none; I'll vouch for them.
Take this from one, my friend, who has the power
To seal accusers' lips.» Get two glass eyes,
And, like these rotten charlatans, pretend
To see the things you don't.—Now, now, now, now.
Pull off my boots. Harder, harder—there.

EDGAR
[aside] O, substance and absurdity combined!
Reason in madness!

LEAR
If you desire to mourn my fate, then take
My eyes. I know you well enough. You're Gloucester.
You must be calm. We entered this place crying.
You know, the first time that we smell the air
We wail and cry. I'll preach to you. Now listen.

[LEAR removes his makeshift crown]

GLOUCESTER
Look what's become of us!

LEAR
When we are born, we cry that we have come
To this great stage of fools—A good design. [studying his
    makeshift crown]
It was a cunning stratagem to shoe
A horse brigade with felt. I'll test it out.
And when I've crept up on these sons-in-law,   185
Then kill, kill, kill, kill, kill, kill!

   [Enter a GENTLEMAN, with ATTENDANTS]

GENTLEMAN (serving Cordelia)
O, here he is. Grab hold of him.—O, Sir,
Your dearest daughter—

LEAR
No rescuers? What, a prisoner? I am fortune's
Complete and true-born plaything. Treat me well.   190
You'll get a ransom. Let me have a surgeon;
My brain is cut.

GENTLEMAN
            Whatever you desire.

LEAR
No helpers? Just myself?
Why, this would make a man a man of tears,
Whose eyes are used as garden water-pots,   195
⟨Yes, and to dampen autumn dust.⟩
I will die boldly, like a spruced up bridegroom.
Yes! I'll be jovial. Come, come, I am a king,
Masters, don't you know that?

GENTLEMAN
You are a royal one, and we obey you.   200

LEAR
Then there's hope yet. Come on, if you get me, you must get
me by running. Tally-ho, tally-ho!

   [Exit running. ATTENDANTS follow]

GENTLEMAN
A sight so pitiful in the lowest wretch—
Unspeakable in kings. His daughter will
Redeem us from the universal curse   205
That pair have placed upon us.

EDGAR
Hail, noble sir.

GENTLEMAN
    God bless you. What's your wish?

EDGAR
Have you heard news, sir, of a coming battle?

GENTLEMAN
Indeed, and it is widely-known to all
Whose ears distinguish sound.

EDGAR
                       If I may ask,   210
How near's the other army?

GENTLEMAN
Nearby and marching fast. The main advance
Should reach here any hour.

EDGAR
I thank you sir, that's all.

GENTLEMAN
Although the queen's here on a special mission,   215
Her army has moved on.

EDGAR
                    I thank you, sir.

[Exit GENTLEMAN]

GLOUCESTER
You ever-gentle gods, take my breath from me.
Don't let my darker side tempt me again
To die before you wish it!

EDGAR
               A good prayer, father.

GLOUCESTER
Now, good sir, who are you?   220

EDGAR
A quite poor man, resigned to fortune's blows
Who, due to sorrows both observed and suffered,
Is prone to feeling pity. Give me your hand,
I'll lead you to some lodgings.

GLOUCESTER
                A hearty thanks.

The bounty and the blessings of the heavens, 225
With booty to boot.

[Enter OSWALD]

OSWALD
What luck! A reward!
Your eyeless head was first conceived in flesh
To raise my fortunes. You old, malicious traitor,
Quickly make peace with heaven. The sword is drawn
That will destroy you.

GLOUCESTER.
Now let your welcome hand 230
Have strength enough to do it.

[EDGAR steps between them]

OSWALD
Why, bold peasant,
Do you defend this wanted traitor? Go,
Before the sickness of his fortunes takes
A similar hold on you. Release his arm.

EDGAR
[rustic stage dialect] No letting go, sir, 'cept there's
  further 'casion.[5] 235

OSWALD
Let go, slave, or you die!

EDGAR
Good gentleman, go along with you, and let poor folk pass.
If bullying could snap the life from me, I'd a' not held onto
it as long as a week. Nay, keep wide of the old man. Keep
away's my warning, or I'll test whether your noggin or my 240
cudgel is the harder. I mean it.

OSWALD
Draw, dunghill!

[They fight]

EDGAR
I'll pick your teeth with it, sir. Come on! Your jabs don't
put the fright in me.

[They fight, and OSWALD falls]

OSWALD
Slave, you have slain me. Peasant, take my purse,
And if you hope to thrive, bury my body,
And give the letters which you'll find on me
To Edmund Earl of Gloucester. Look for him
Among the British faction. O, untimely death!
Death!

[OSWALD dies]

EDGAR
I know you well, an all-too-willing servant,
No less obedient to your lady's vices
Than badness would demand.

GLOUCESTER
                    What, is he dead?

EDGAR
Sit down now, father. Rest yourself—
Let's check these pockets. The letters that he speaks of
May be my friends. He's dead; I'm only sorry
That I'm his executioner. Let's see—
Permit me, gentle wax; excuse these manners.
To know our enemies' minds, we rip their hearts.
To rip their papers is more lawful. [breaks the seal]

[reads the letter] *"Let our mutual vows be remembered.
You have many opportunities to remove him. If you do
not lack the desire, the time and place will be fruitfully
arranged. Nothing can be done if he returns a conqueror.
Then I will be the prisoner and his bed my jail. Deliver
me from that loathèd warmth and assume his place for
your labors. Your—I wish I could say 'wife'— affectionate
servant, pledged to risk all for you.*
                                Goneril."

The unmapped regions of a woman's lust! 270
A plot upon her virtuous husband's life,
And the reward my brother!—I'll scrape some sand
Across you, you unholy messenger
For murderous lechers; and when the time is ripe
I'll use this odious note to daze the eyes 275
Of the death-threatened duke. For him it's good
That I can now report your death and business.

      [Exit EDGAR, dragging out the body]

GLOUCESTER
The king is mad. Yet my vile mind's so stubborn
I still can stand and with such keen awareness
Of my huge sorrows! Better to be crazy. 280
My thoughts would then be severed from my grief;
My woes, wrapped in delusion, would soon lose
All knowledge of themselves.

      [Enter EDGAR]

EDGAR
                Give me your hand.

      [A distant drum]

Far off I seem to hear a beating drum.
Come, father, I will lodge you with a friend. 285

      [Exit]

Scene Seven. A Tent in the French Camp

      [Enter CORDELIA, KENT (dressed as Caius),
      PHYSICIAN, and a GENTLEMAN][6]

CORDELIA
Good Kent, how can I live and work enough
To match your goodness? My life will be too short
And every measure fails.

KENT
To be acknowledged, mam, is overpayment.
Reports of me should state the simple facts,   5
Not stretched or trimmed, just true.

CORDELIA
                         Let's dress you better.
These clothes are memories of times much worse.
I hope you'll change them now.

KENT
                         Indulge me, madam.
To show myself now shortens my fixed aim.   10
I ask one favor: Don't say who I am
Until the time is fitting.

CORDELIA
So be it, my good lord. [to the Physician] How is the king?

PHYSICIAN
Quietly sleeping, madam.

CORDELIA
                         O kind gods,
Mend the great breach in this mistreated being!   15
Restring the jarring, untuned faculties
Of this child-transformed father!

PHYSICIAN
                         May we, your majesty,
If you please, wake the king from his long sleep.

CORDELIA
Judge based upon your knowledge, and proceed
In line with that decision. Is he dressed?   20

GENTLEMAN
Yes, madam. While the king was soundly sleeping,
We put fresh garments on him.

PHYSICIAN
Please stay close by, good madam, when we wake him.
His self-control concerns me.

‹CORDELIA
                    Very well.›

[Enter LEAR, sleeping, in a chair carried
           by SERVANTS. Soft music]

‹PHYSICIAN
Come closer, please.—And play the music louder!›   25

CORDELIA
[kissing Lear] O my dear father! Restoration, place
Your medicine on my lips, and let this kiss
Repair the violent harm that my two sisters
Have done to one they should revere!

KENT
                    Kind princess!

CORDELIA
Had you not been their father, these white locks   30
Would have demanded pity. Was this a face
To be sent out against the jarring winds?
‹To stand against the deep dread voice of thunder?
Beneath the terrible and darting stroke
Of crisscrossed lightning? Standing watch alone   35
With this thin helmet?› [touches his balding head] My
     enemy's dog,
If he had bit me, could have spent that night
Beside my fire. Yet you preferred, poor father,
To share a hole with swine and cast-off tramps
And bits of moldy straw. How could this be?   40
A miracle your life and mind right then
Did not expire.—He's waking. Speak to him.

PHYSICIAN
You speak, ma'am. It's more fitting.

CORDELIA
How is my royal lord? How is your majesty?

LEAR
You do me wrong to pull me from the grave. 45
Though you're a soul in heaven, I am strapped
Upon a wheel of fire so that my tears
Will scald like molten lead.

CORDELIA
                Sir, do you know me?

LEAR
You are a spirit, I see. Where did you die?

CORDELIA
[to the others] Still, still, far off! 50

PHYSICIAN
He's just woke up. Leave him alone awhile.

LEAR
Where have I been? Where am I? Bright daylight?
I'm terribly deluded. I'd surely die from pity
If others suffered this. I don't know what to say.
I will not swear these are my hands. Let's see. 55
I feel this pinprick. If I could be sure
Of my condition!

CORDELIA
            O, look upon me, sir,
And hold your hands in blessing over me.
No, sir, you must not kneel.

LEAR
              Please, do not mock me:
I'm an old man, who's senile and quite foolish, 60
Eighty and upward, not an hour more nor less,
And, to speak frankly,
I fear that I am not in my right mind.

I feel I should know you and know this man,
Yet I'm uneasy, for I'm entirely ignorant   65
Of where I am and have no memory
Of any of these garments, nor do I know
What place I lodged last night. Don't laugh at me,
But I swear as a man, I think this lady
Must be my child Cordelia.

CORDELIA
                    And so I am. I am.   70

LEAR
Are your tears wet? Indeed, they are. Don't weep.
If you have poison for me, I will drink it.
I know you do not love me, for your sisters,
If I remember right, have done me wrong.
You have good cause, they don't.

CORDELIA
                    No cause, no cause.   75

LEAR
Am I in France?

KENT
           In your own kingdom, sir.

LEAR
Do not play tricks on me.

PHYSICIAN
Be comforted, good madam. The great frenzy,
You see, has died in him, ⟨and yet it's dangerous
To make him go back over time he's lost.⟩   80
Urge him to go in. Trouble him no more
Until his mind has settled.

CORDELIA
Would walking please your highness?

LEAR
You must bear with me. If you would, forget and forgive. I
am old and foolish.   85

[Exit LEAR, CORDELIA, PHYSICIAN,
and ATTENDANTS]

⟨**GENTLEMAN**
Is it confirmed, sir, that the Duke of Cornwall was slain?

KENT
Quite certain, sir.

GENTLEMAN
Who is the leader of his people?

KENT
Word is, it's the bastard son of Gloucester.

GENTLEMAN
They say Edgar, his banished son, is with the Earl of Kent   90
in Germany.

KENT
Reports have varied. It's time to be on guard. The armed
forces of the kingdom are approaching quickly.

GENTLEMAN
The showdown is likely to be bloody. Farewell, sir.

[Exit]

KENT
The mark that ends this sentence that I write   95
Grows ill or well today as armies fight.

[Exit]⟩

King Lear

Act Five

Act Five

Scene One. The British Camp near Dover

[Enter, with drum and colors, EDMUND, REGAN, GENTLEMEN, SOLDIERS, and others]

EDMUND
[to a Gentleman] Learn from the duke if his most recent plan
Still holds or if he's been induced again
To change his mind. He's full of vacillation
And self-reproach. Bring back a firm decision.

[To an OFFICER, who goes out]

REGAN
My sister's servant surely met misfortune. 5

EDMUND
I fear it too, my lady.

REGAN
Now, sweet lord, [moves out of hearing of the soldiers]
You know the good things I intend for you.
Tell me—now truly—I must get the truth,
Do you not love my sister?

EDMUND
Honorably.

REGAN
And you have never traced her husband's path 10
To the forbidden place?

⟨**EDMUND**
>>>>>>>>>>>>>>>>Your thoughts deceive you.

REGAN
I'm fearful that you two have been in touch
And heart to heart—and in the fullest sense.⟩

EDMUND
No, on my honor, madam.

REGAN
No longer can I stand her. My dear lord,   15
Don't be too cozy with her.

EDMUND
>>>>>>>>>>>>>>Trust me, lady—
She and the duke are here!

[Enter, with drum and colors, ALBANY,
GONERIL, and SOLDIERS]

⟨**GONERIL**
[aside] I'd rather lose the battle than to let
Her shake him loose from me.⟩

ALBANY
Our very loving sister, good you're here.   20
Sir, this I heard—the king came to his daughter,
With others who've been forced by our harsh rule
Into dissent. ⟨When I cannot act nobly,
I never can be valiant. This affair
Concerns us, for as France invades our land,   25
We must face him and not the king or those
With just and serious grievances against us.[1]

EDMUND
Sir, you speak nobly.⟩

REGAN
>>>>>>>>>>>>>Why discuss this now?

GONERIL
Combine as one against the enemy,
For these domestic, personal disputes   30
Are not the issue here.

ALBANY
                    Then let's assemble
Our senior warriors and devise a plan.

‹EDMUND
[to Albany] I'll see you in a moment in your tent.›

REGAN
Sister, you'll go with us? [sensing that Edmund and Goneril are lagging behind]

GONERIL
No.   35

REGAN
It's quite appropriate. Please, go with us.

GONERIL
[aside] O, ho, I get the drift.—[aloud] Yes, I will go.

        [As they exit, enter EDGAR, disguised]

EDGAR
If your grace ever spoke with one so poor,
Then listen to one word.

ALBANY
                    I'll catch up.—Speak.

    [Exit EDMUND, REGAN, GONERIL, OFFICERS,
            SOLDIERS, and ATTENDANTS]

EDGAR
Before you fight the battle, read this letter.   40
If you're victorious, let the trumpet call

The one that brought it. Ragged though I seem,
I can produce a knight who'll prove in combat
The truth of what's claimed there. If you go down,
Your interest in this world will end as well   45
And all plots cease. May fortune favor you! [hands
   Albany the letter]

ALBANY
Stay till I've read the letter.

EDGAR
                    I was forbid to.
When the time's right, just let your herald call me,
And I'll appear again.

ALBANY
Well then, farewell. I will read through your letter. 50

            [Exit EDGAR]
            [Re-enter EDMUND]

EDMUND
The enemy's in view. Amass your forces.
[hands Albany a paper] Here is a guess of their true
   strength and numbers
From diligent surveillance. And it's urgent
That you move fast.

ALBANY
               We'll be in place in time.

                [Exit]

EDMUND
To both these sisters I have sworn my love,   55
Each watchful of the other, as those bitten
Are of the adder. Which of them shall I take?
Both? One? Or neither? Neither can be enjoyed
If both remain alive. To take the widow
Exasperates and drives her sister mad,   60
And it is hard to realize my ambitions

While Albany's alive. It's clear we'll need
His face to lead this battle. After that,
She can arrange, since she would like him gone,
His speedy rubbing out. As for the pardon   65
Which he intends for Lear and for Cordelia—
After the fight, and they are in our power,
They'll never see such mercy, for my fate
Obliges me to act, not join debate.

[Exit]

Scene Two. A Field Between the Two Camps

[Trumpet call to arms. LEAR, CORDELIA, and their
FORCES enter with drums and colors,
cross the stage, and exit]]
[Enter EDGAR and GLOUCESTER]

EDGAR
Your honor, use the shadow of this tree
To shelter you. Pray that the righteous thrive.
If ever I return to you again,
I'll bring you comfort.

GLOUCESTER
                Grace go with you, sir!

[Exit EDGAR].
[Trumpet call for retreat. Re-enter EDGAR]

EDGAR
Let's go, old man—give me your hand—Lets' go!   5
King Lear has lost, he and his daughter captured.
Give me your hand. Come on!

GLOUCESTER
No further. I can drop and rot right here.

EDGAR
What, more ill thoughts again? Men must endure
Their leaving here just as they did their coming.   10
The time is ripening—that's what matters now.

«GLOUCESTER
That's true too.»

[Exit]

Scene Three. The British Camp near Dover

[Enter, in conquest, with drum and colors,
EDMUND, CAPTAIN, OFFICERS, SOLDIERS;
LEAR and CORDELIA are prisoners]

EDMUND
Some of you men, take them out. Guard them well
Until the higher ranks give us clear word
On what their sentence is.

CORDELIA
                          We're not the first
With pure intent who have incurred the worst.
It's your distress, my king, that casts me down.   5
Were it just me, I'd out-scowl fickle fortune.
Shouldn't we face these daughters and these sisters?

LEAR
No, no, no, no! Come, let's go off to prison.
We two alone will sing like caged-up birds,
And when you ask my blessing, I'll kneel down   10
And ask of you forgiveness. Then we'll live,
And pray, and sing, and tell old tales, and laugh
At dolled-up butterflies, and hear poor rogues
Talk of court news, and we'll talk with them too—

Who loses and who wins, who's in, who's out— 15
Pretend to know the mystery of things,[2]
As if we were God's spies. And we'll outlast,
In a walled prison, gangs and cliques of great ones
That ebb and flow with moons.

EDMUND
                     Take them away.

LEAR
Upon such sacrifices, my Cordelia, 20
The gods themselves toss incense. Do I have you?
Who parts us, he must bring a torch from heaven
And smoke us out like foxes. Wipe your eyes.
The bad witch shall devour them, meat and skin,[3]
Before they'll make us weep. We'll see 'em starve first. 25
Come.

    [Exit LEAR and CORDELIA, under guard]

EDMUND
Come this way, captain. Listen. [gives him a paper]
Take this note with you. Follow them to prison.
One rank I have advanced you. If you do
As this instructs you, you are on the path 30
To noble status. Understand—since men
Bend with the times, and being tender-hearted
Does not befit a warrior—your great mission
Will not allow discussion. Say you'll do it,
Or thrive by other means.

CAPTAIN (follower of Edmund)
                    My lord, I'll do it. 35

EDMUND
Get to it and feel lucky when you're through.
Read this—at once, I say. Arrange it just
As I've described it.

⟨**CAPTAIN**
I cannot pull a cart or eat dried oats.
If it is man's work, I will do it.⟩ 40

[Exit CAPTAIN]
[Flourish. Enter ALBANY, GONERIL, REGAN,
OFFICERS, and ATTENDANTS]

ALBANY
Sir, you have shown today your valiant lineage,
And fate has led you well. You've taken captive
Those who were enemies in this day's strife.
Please turn them over now so we can find
A treatment that will weigh what they deserve 45
Against our needs for safety.

EDMUND
⸺⸺⸺⸺⸺⸺⸺⸺Sir, I thought it fit
To put into confinement under guard
The miserable old king who has the age—
And even more the title—to bewitch
And draw the masses' favor to his side 50
And turn our conscripts pikes back toward the eyes
Of our commanders. With him I sent the queen,
My reason quite the same, and they are ready
Tomorrow, or thereafter, to appear
Where you convene your hearing. ⟨At this time 55
We sweat and bleed. When friends have lost their friends,
A cause, though just, till passions cool, is cursed
By those who feel its sting.
The question of Cordelia and her father
Requires a calmer setting.⟩

ALBANY
⸺⸺⸺⸺⸺⸺⸺⸺If I may, 60
I see you as my subject in this war,
Not as a peer.

REGAN
⸺⸺⸺⸺⸺That's how I choose to rank him.

It seems my wishes might have been reviewed
Before you spoke so soon. He led our troops,
Carried the mandate of my rank and person,
And as my second-in-command may stand   65
And call himself your equal.

GONERIL
                    Not so fast.
He's elevated more by his own merits,
Than titles you bestow.

REGAN
                   By granting him
These powers, he is equal to the best.   70

ALBANY
He'd have them all were he to marry you.[4]

REGAN
How often fools are prophets.

GONERIL
                  Heavens! Heavens!
How hard you squint to see through jealous eyes.

REGAN
[sick to her stomach] Lady, I am not well, or I would
    answer
With anger flooding from me.—[to Edmund] General,   75
Take all my soldiers, prisoners, inheritance.
«Dispose of them, and me; these walls, they're yours.»
Witness this, world, that I appoint you now
My lord and master.

        [They rise as queen and king,
        with EDMUND supporting her]

GONERIL
                Intending to enjoy him?

ALBANY
The power to say no's not left to you. 80

EDMUND
Nor you, lord.

ALBANY
      Yes, it is, half-noble fellow.

REGAN
[to Edmund] Let the drum strike, and claim my title
  yours.

ALBANY
Slow down and listen.—Edmund, I arrest you.
The charge? High treason, along with your accuser,
This gilded snake. [points to Goneril] [then to Regan] As
  for your claim, fair sister, 85
I bar it in the interest of my wife.
She has subleased herself out to this lord,
And I, her husband, call off your engagement.
If you must marry, then you should court me.
My lady's spoken for.

«GONERIL
      It's now a farce! 90

ALBANY»
You are armed, Gloucester—let the trumpet sound.
If no one else appears to demonstrate
Your heinous, manifest, and many treasons,
Here is my challenge. [throwing down a glove] I'll prove
  it to your heart,
Before I eat, that you're on every point 95
No less than I've asserted.

REGAN
      Sick, O, sick!

GONERIL
[aside] If not, I'll never trust a drug.

EDMUND
There's my reply [throwing down a glove]. Whoever in this world
Calls me a traitor is a lying rogue.
Call with your trumpet. He who dares approach,
To him, to you, whoever, I'll uphold
My truth and honor firmly.

ALBANY
                    A herald, ho!

[Enter a HERALD]

[to Edmund] Your valor's single-handed, for your soldiers,
All mustered in my name, have in my name
Now been discharged.

REGAN
                    Inside my sickness grows.

ALBANY
She is not well. Convey her to my tent.

[REGAN is helped to exit]

Herald, come here.—And let the trumpet sound—
Read it outloud.

«OFFICER
Sound, trumpet!»   [A trumpet sounds]

HERALD
[Reads] *"If any man of gentleman's rank or higher enlisted in the army wishes to maintain that Edmund, supposed Earl of Gloucester, is a traitor many times over, let him appear by the third sound of the trumpet. Edmund is firm in his defense."*

HERALD
Sound! [first trumpet sounds] 115
Again! [second trumpet sounds]
Again! [third trumpet sounds]

[Trumpet answers from a distance]
[Enter EDGAR, in armor, preceded by a trumpet]

ALBANY
Ask him his business here, why he appears
At the third trumpet's call.

HERALD
                   State who you are,
Your name, your rank, and why you're answering 120
This summons.

EDGAR (disguised by armor)
              Understand, my name is lost,
Gnawed bare and cankerous by treachery's tooth.
Yet I'm as noble as the adversary
I've come to meet.

ALBANY
              Who is that adversary?

EDGAR
Who here will speak for Edmund, Earl of Gloucester? 125

EDMUND
I'm he. What will you tell him?

EDGAR
                  Draw your sword,
And if my words malign a noble heart,
Your arm will give you justice. Here is mine. [draws his
   sword]
Behold, it is the privilege of my rank
My oath, and my profession. I declare— 130
Despite your strength, youth, office, and renown,

Despite your victor's sword and new-fired fortune,
Your valor and your courage—you're a traitor,
False to your gods, your brother, and your father,
Who plots against this high illustrious prince, 135
And who from that point topmost on your head
Down to the depths and dust beneath your foot,
Is spotted like a toad with treason. Say "no,"
This sword, this arm, and every fiber will
Be poised to prove the heart to which I speak 140
Is lying.

EDMUND
It's proper that I ask your name,
«But since your outer looks are fair and warlike,»
And as your tongue conveys some trace of breeding,
I will disdain and spurn the rules of knighthood,
Which do, to be precise, permit delay. 145
So back I toss these treasons in your face
These hellish lies which inundate your heart,
And since my words glance off and hardly bruise,
This sword of mine must carve an instant path
To where they'll rest forever.—Trumpets, speak! 150

[Trumpets sound. They fight. EDMUND falls. EDGAR places his sword at EDMUND's throat to kill him]

ALBANY
Spare him, spare him!

GONERIL
This is trickery, Gloucester.
The laws of war do not force you to answer
An unknown challenger. You are not vanquished,
But cheated and beguiled.

ALBANY
Shut your mouth, woman,
Or I will plug it with this paper.—Wait, sir. 155
[to Goneril] You, worse than any name, read your own

evil.
Don't tear it. I can see you recognize it.

[Shows the letter to EDMUND]

GONERIL
And say I do—I am the law, not you.
Who would arraign me for it?

ALBANY
                    Monstrous! O!
D'you recognize it?

GONERIL
            Don't ask what I know.

[Exit]

ALBANY
[to an Officer, who exits] Go after her. She's lost control.
   Restrain her.

EDMUND
All of these things you've charged me with I've done,
And more, much more, and time will bring it out.
It's done, and so am I. But who are you
Who's triumphed over me? If your blood's noble,
Then I forgive you.

EDGAR
            Let's exchange forgiveness.
It's no less noble than your blood is, Edmund.
If more, then all the more you've wronged me.
My name is Edgar, and your father's son.
The gods are just and make our wicked pleasures
Their instruments to plague us.
The dark and sinful place where you were made
Cost him his eyes.

EDMUND
                Your words are right. It's true;
The wheel has come full circle. Here I am.

ALBANY
Your stride itself implied to me what seemed
A royal nobleness. I must embrace you.
Let sorrow split my heart to think that I
Could hate you or your father!

EDGAR
                      Worthy prince,
I understand.

ALBANY
             Where have you hid yourself?
How did you learn about your father's wounds?

EDGAR
By nursing them, my lord. Hear this brief tale.
And once it's told, O if my heart would burst!
In order to escape the bloody warrant
That hounded me so closely—life's so sweet
We'd rather feel the pain of death each hour
Than die at once—I forced myself to change
Into a madman's rags, assume a semblance
That even dogs disdained, and in this guise,
I met my father with his bleeding rings—
Their precious stones just lost— became his guide,
Led him, begged for him, saved him from despair.
Never—O error!—revealed myself to him
Till one half hour ago, when I was armed.
Not sure, though hoping he could benefit,
I asked his blessing, and from first to last
Described our pilgrimage. But sad to say,
His damaged heart, too weak to bear the pull
Of passion's two extremes, of joy and grief—
Burst as it smiled.

EDMUND
                This tale of yours has moved me
And will perhaps do good. But please speak on.
You look as if there's more you wish to say.

ALBANY
If there is more, more woeful, hold it in,
For I am nearly ready to dissolve
Just hearing this.

‹EDGAR
                Good place to stick a period
For those who don't love sorrow. To add another,
To amplify too much, would just make more,
And pass beyond all limits.
While I was mourning loudly, a man came there
Who, having seen me in my lowest state,
Shunned my repugnant company, but when
He saw who'd suffered this, with his strong arms
He held me by the neck and bellowed out
As if to burst the sky, fell toward my father,
Told the most poignant tale of Lear and him
That ears have ever heard, and in recounting,
His grief grew powerful and the strings of life
Began to snap. When trumpets sounded twice,
I left him in a trance.

ALBANY
                But who was this?

EDGAR
Kent, sir, the banished Kent, who in disguise
Followed his hostile king, performing duties
Too lowly for a slave.›

[A GENTLEMAN rushes in with a bloody knife]

GENTLEMAN
Help, help! O, help!

EDGAR
                What kind of help?

《ALBANY
                        Speak, man.》

EDGAR
Explain this bloody knife.

GENTLEMAN
                It's warm, it's steaming.
It just came from the heart of—O! she's dead!

ALBANY
Who's dead? Speak, man.   225

GENTLEMAN
Your wife, sir, your wife. And her sister was poisoned by her. She confessed it.

EDMUND
I was betrothed to both of them. All three
Now marry in an instant.

《EDGAR
                Here comes Kent.》

                [Enter KENT]

ALBANY
Produce the bodies, whether dead or living.   230

                [Exit GENTLEMAN]

This judgment of the heavens, which makes us tremble,
Passed sentenced without pity. [referring to Kent] Is he
  the one?
This crisis won't allow the usual welcome
That simple manners call for.

KENT
             I have come
To bid my last farewell to king and master.   235
Is he not here?

ALBANY
          The biggest thing forgotten!
Talk, Edmund. Where's the king? And where's Cordelia?

   [The bodies of GONERIL and REGAN are brought in]

Look at this sight, Kent.

KENT
Lord, what's all this?

EDMUND
             Still, Edmund was beloved.
One poisoned by the other for my sake,   240
And then she slew herself.

ALBANY
No doubt correct. Cover their faces.

EDMUND
A few gasps left. I want to do some good,
In spite of my own nature. Quickly go—
In all haste—to the castle. Rescind my order   245
To end the lives of Lear and his Cordelia.
Stop this in time.

ALBANY
          Run, run, O, run!

EDGAR
But where, my lord?—Whose order is this? Send
Some symbol of your office.

EDMUND
Of course. [to Edgar] Here, take my sword and give it to   250
The Captain.[6]

ALBANY
        Quickly, there are lives at stake.

[Exit EDGAR]

EDMUND
He has instructions from your wife and me
To hang Cordelia in the prison and
To lay the blame upon her own despair
And claim she took her life. 255

ALBANY
The gods defend her!—Take him out for now.

[EDMUND is carried out]
[Re-enter LEAR, with CORDELIA dead in his arms; EDGAR, OFFICER, and others following]

LEAR
Howl, howl, howl, howl!—O, you are men of stone!
If I possessed your tongues and eyes, I'd crack
The sphere of heaven with them. She's gone forever.
I know when one is dead and when one lives. 260
She's dead as earth. Lend me a looking glass.
For if her breath still mists the mirror, why then
She lives.

KENT
        Is this the promised end of time?

EDGAR
Or just that horror's likeness?

ALBANY
        [looking heavenward] Fall and cease this!

LEAR
This feather stirs—she lives. If it is so, 265
It is a stroke of luck which will repay
All sorrows I have felt.

KENT
          O my good master! [Kneeling]

LEAR
O please, away.

EDGAR
          It's noble Kent, your friend.

LEAR
A plague upon you, murderers, traitors all!
I might have saved her. Now she's gone for ever!
Cordelia, Cordelia! Stay a little. Ha!
What's that you say? Her voice was oh so soft,
Gentle, and low—an excellent thing in women.
I killed that wretch who I caught hanging you.

OFFICER
It's true, my lords, he did.

LEAR
          Didn't I, fellow?
I've seen days when my saber bit so deep
It would have made him leap. I am old now,
And all these troubles wreck me.—Who are you?
My eyes are not the best—give me a second.

KENT
If fate could boast of two first loved then hated,
We're looking at one now.

LEAR
My eyes are fading. Aren't you Kent?

KENT
          I am,
Your servant Kent.—Where is your servant Caius?

LEAR
He's a good fellow, I can tell you that.
He'll fight, and quickly too. He's dead and rotten.

KENT
No, my good lord. I'm one and the same man…

LEAR
[distracted] I'll see to that soon.

KENT
…Who from the start of your change for the worse
Has followed your sad steps…

LEAR
You're welcome here.

KENT
…And no one else—All's cheerless, dark, and deathly— 290
Your eldest daughters have destroyed themselves,
And in despair are dead.

LEAR
Yes, I think so.

ALBANY
He knows not what he says. It's futile now
To introduce ourselves to him.

EDGAR
Quite useless.

[Enter an OFFICER]

OFFICER
Edmund is dead, my lord.

ALBANY
At this point but a trifle. 295
You lords and noble friends, here's my intention.
What aid there is to ease his great decline
Will be administered. Me? I'll resign,
For while there's life in this old sovereign,
I yield him all my power. [to Edgar and Kent] To you
your rights, 300

Plus proceeds and such titles as your honor
Has more than earned for you. —All friends will taste
The wages of their virtue, and all foes
Will get the cup that they deserve.—What's this?

LEAR
My little fool is hanged! No, no, no life! 305
Why should a dog, a horse, a rat, have life
And you no breath at all? You'll come no more,
Never, never, never, never, never!
Would you undo this button? Thank you, sir.
《Do you see this? Look at her! Look! Her lips! 310
Look there, look there!》

[LEAR dies]

EDGAR
He's fainted!—My lord, my lord!

KENT
Break, heart. I beg you, break!

EDGAR
Look up, my lord.

KENT
Don't taunt his spirit. Let him go! He'd hate
Whoever on the rack of this rough world
Stretched him out longer.

EDGAR
He is gone indeed. 315

KENT
A wonder that he could endure so long.
He lived on stolen time.

ALBANY
Carry them out. Our pressing business now
Is public grief. [to Kent and Edgar] You two friends of my
  soul,
Go rule and make this wounded kingdom whole. 320

KENT
I have a journey, sir, and soon will go.
My master calls me—I must not say no.

EDGAR
We must accept the weight of this sad day,
Voice what we feel, not what we ought to say.
The oldest bore the most; we who are young   325
Will never see so much, nor live so long.

        [Exit ALL, with a funeral march]

The End

Endnotes

Act One

[1] There is no consensus on the original line's meaning, "All other joys/ Which the most precious square of sense possesses (Folio: 'professes')." "Square" could mean a carpenter's square, or "square of sense" could figuratively refer to the body. Neither seems obvious, so I have carried on the accounting and real estate puns that appear throughout the scene, with square having the sense of "just proportion" or "regulation."

[2] The Folio has the more common "Nothing will come of nothing." But the Quarto's "Nothing can come of nothing" is more blasphemous and reveals Lear's tendency to speak carelessly. Since modern audiences probably miss the blasphemy, "Nothing will come of nothing" may be the more dramatic choice if the actor sees Lear as already losing his temper. I sense he loses it several lines later.

[3] In my translation, Lear calls on Kent to drop the matter, but Kent presses on, switching to direct language. In another interpretation, Lear tells Kent to come to the point. Kent says that he would only speak bluntly if he thought Lear had lost his mind. Here is a translation favoring that view (original in parentheses).

> *Lear*: Your bow is bent and drawn; release the shaft.
>   (The bow is bent and drawn; make from the shaft)
> *Kent*: I'd rather drop it, though its barbs invade
>   (Let it fall rather, though the fork invade)
>   The tissues of my heart. Kent would be blunt
>   (The region of my heart: be Kent unmannerly)
>   If Lear were mad. What would you do, old man?
>   (When Lear is mad. What wouldst thou do, old man?)

This second interpretation requires a nonce usage of "make from" to mean "release" or "let fly." Note that Kent does not keep his composure for long since he raises the issue of Lear's madness and insults the king by saying "thou" and "old man." Here is a third translation where Kent begins diplomatically but becomes angry.

> *Kent*: I'd rather let it drop and have its barbs
>   Invade my heart. But I must now be blunt
>   If Lear is mad. What would you do, old man?

[4] The much-disputed original reads "...and must be used/With checks as flatteries—when they are seen abused." Another possible translation is "...that we must praise/ With reprimands when flattery's abused."

Act Two

[1] The original lines ("Goose, an I had you upon Sarum plain,/I'd drive ye cackling home to Camelot.") have unexplained references to Sarum (Salisbury) Plain and Camelot. I designed an insult which brings attention to Oswald's quaking with fear.

[2] The original ("though I should win your displeasure to entreat me to't") seems uninterpretable. Here's another translation: "Even if I could get your 'Dis-grace' to beg me to be one."

[3] Scholars have several takes on the original ("None of these rogues and cowards/But Ajax is their fool"). My translation works as a defense against Oswald's charges. Another interpretation sees the line as an insult to Cornwall. Here is a possible translation: "These rogues and cowards/All fool this reeking braggart."

[4] The original "Would with his daughter speak, come and tends service" makes little sense and has been corrected in several ways ("command her service" or "commands, tends service," or even "commands true service"). My translation has Lear stating plainly and forcefully, without cleverness or irony, what he expects of his daughter.

[5] Lear's speech, as true of many in this scene, becomes metrically quite complex and strained with short and long lines, epic caesuras, and extra syllables. As I have done throughout the play, I keep the original metrical pattern intact, acknowledging that Shakespeare had a dramatic purpose for these choices.

Act Three

[1] There are three versions of Kent's speech. The Quarto omits lines 22-29. The Folio omits lines 30-42. Most modern editions include all the lines. Some scholars say that the Folio lines (22-29) were meant to replace, not add to, the Quarto lines (30-42), arguing that the longer speech seems dramatically incoherent, redundant, and rambling. France, of course, had to have planned the invasion long before Lear wandered into the storm. However, my translation allows enough ambiguity in France's plans to avoid any absurd distortion of time. Kent's behavior is consistent with his loquaciousness in other scenes. The Folio, by the way, deletes most discussion of the French invasion.

[2] This rhymed prophecy has several variants. Lines 90-91 often appear after line 84. A view I adopted in the first edition of this translation has lines 92-93 following line 84. That version implies that corruption is the usual situation since walking on feet is the normal state of affairs. The utopian stanza then ends with a prediction of chaos.

[3] The original reads "Dolphin, my boy, boy, sessa!" No paraphrase has been agreed on. I take it to be lunatic instructions to a hunting dog named Dolphin, an alternate pronunciation of Dauphin. Perhaps the name bears a loose phonetic resemblance to "the fiend." Several times

previously Edgar's Poor Tom responded to the sound, not the meaning, of words. "Sessa" could mean "cease."

⁴ The original line ("but a provoking merit, set a-work by a reproveable badness in himself") has prompted several interpretations. One alternative is "…but rather just provocation, prompted by a reprehensible badness in the Earl himself." Another possibility is "but rather a virtuous quality brought to light by a reprehensible badness in the Earl himself."

⁵ The original is the uninterpretable line "All cruels else subscribed." Debate concerns whether the line is part of the quotation spoken to the imagined doorkeeper, whether "cruels" means cruel deeds or cruel creatures, or whether the Quarto's "subscribe" or the Folio's "subscribed" is correct. Another interpretation might get this translation: "Forget your other cruelties…but I'll see."

Act Four

¹ The original is disputed ("parti-eyd" vs. "poorlie, leed"). Edgar seems more likely to notice his father's eyes (perhaps with a gory description) than to comment on the age and standing of his guide. But here is a translation that scans in case the second, and more common, interpretation is preferred:

> …Is this my father?
> Led by this one poor man?

² Some texts have the line read "My fool usurps my body." The dispute concerns how to correct the Quarto's mysterious "My foote usurps my body."

³ The original ("Marry, your manhood mew—") has several interpretations. Some see a cat's meow mocking Albany. Some see a play on the word "mew" from falconry, meaning to keep under restraint. My translation aims for both meanings.

⁴ This line (originally, "Nature's above art in that respect") is open to many interpretations: natural strength is superior to skill, it is better to be the king who makes the coins than to be the image on it, a born king can never lose his natural rights, a born king is superior to any counterfeit king. My translation emphasizes a literal comparison of the real king and his image on the coin, yet leaves room for the less literal interpretations while playing into the debate in Shakespeare's day over the conflict between art and nature.

⁵ Edgar in the original slips into a stereotypical stage dialect. I supply a folksy equivalent.

⁶ The Quarto has Lear already present, lying on a bed asleep. The Folio

has him carried in after line 23 as if being restored to his throne (and health, Cordelia hopes).

Act Five

[1] Lines 23–27 (from "When I..." on) were not in the Folio. Many scholars feel the original lines 25-26 were garbled in the Quarto with possible missing lines and duplicated phrases. ("It toucheth us, as France invades our land,/ Not bolds the king, with others whom, I fear,/ Most just and heavy causes make oppose"). I designed a translation that has Albany reminding the others of who the real threat is. Here are two other plausible translations:.

> Now this affair
> Concerns us some, but France invades our land,
> To give strength to our King and others who
> Have just and serious grievances against us.

And this translation has Albany remind the others why France's invasion must be opposed:

> Now this affair
> Is our concern because our land's invaded
> And not because it gives the King and those
> With just complaints the chance to turn against us.

[2] Another translation is "And keep watch on the mystery of things" or perhaps "And load on us the mystery of things."

[3] Scholars offer many, mostly unconvincing interpretations of the original "The goodyears shall devour them." If "goodyears" refers to time (perhaps a biblical reference to seven good years of harvest turning to seven bad years), then "The good years will turn lean and feast on them" should work. Since Lear may have switched to baby-talk, "bad witch" works if "goodyears" refers to some evil force. If it refers to a disease, then "A cancer will devour them" scans.

[4] Goneril has this line in the Quarto.

[5] In some versions, an officer takes the sword with Edgar staying.

> **EDMUND**
> A good point. [to an Officer] Take my sword
> And give it to the Captain.
>
> **EDGAR**
> Quickly, on your life.   [exit Officer]

Sources

Editions of the Play

The Applause Shakespeare Library: King Lear. 1996. John Russell Brown, ed. London: Applause Books.
The Arden Edition: King Lear. 1901. Kenneth Muir, ed., based on the edition of W.J. Craig. Cambridge: Harvard University Press.
The Bantam Shakespeare: King Lear. 1980. David Bevington, ed. New York: Bantam Books.
Crowell Critical Library: King Lear. 1970. Edward G. Quinn, ed. New York: Thomas Y. Crowell Co.
The Everyman Shakespeare: King Lear. 1991. John F. Andrews, ed. London: J. M. Dent.
The New Folger Library Shakespeare: The Tragedy of King Lear. 1993. New York: Washington Square Press.
The New Penguin Shakespeare: King Lear. 1996. G.K. Hunter, ed. New York: Penguin Books.
A New Variorum Edition of Shakespeare, Vol. 5: King Lear, 2nd ed. 1880. Howard Furness, ed. Philadelphia: J. B. Lippincott & Co.
The Norton Shakespeare: Based on the Oxford Edition, 2nd Edition. 2008, 1997. S. Greenblatt, W. Cohen, J. E. Howard, and K. E. Maus, eds. New York and London: W.W. Norton & Co.
The Pelican Shakespeare: King Lear, the 1608 Quarto and 1623 Folio Texts. 2000. Stephen Orgel, ed. New York: Penguin Books.
The Riverside Shakespeare, 2nd Edition. 1997. Boston: Houghton Mifflin Co.
The RSC Shakespeare. 2007. Jonathan Bate and Eric Rasmussen, eds. New York: The Modern Library.
Shakespeare: Major Plays and the Sonnets. 1948. G.B. Harrison, ed. New York: Harcourt, Brace, and World, inc.

Other Sources

Compact Edition of the Oxford English Dictionary. 1971. Oxford University Press.
Crystal, David and Ben Crystal. *Shakespeare's Words: A Glossary and Language Companion.* 2002. London: Penguin Books.
Onions, C.T. *A Shakespeare Glossary.* 1986. Revised and enlarged by Robert D. Eagleson.
Schmidt, Alexander. 1971. *Shakespeare Lexicon and Quotation Dictionary, Volumes 1 and 2.* New York: Dover Publications.

Facts about King Lear

Shakespeare's 29th play (or so)
Most likely first performed 1605-1606

2,234 blank verse lines (including 64 long lines
and 191 short lines according to George T. Wright's
Shakespeare's Metrical Art)

About 25% prose

19 rhymes and songs

34 speaking parts
3 female speaking parts

The *Internet Movie Database* list 21 films with the title *King Lear,* dating back to 1916, including the *Yiddish King Lear* (1934). One of the most memorable adaptations is Akira Kurosawa's *Ran* (1985). Is the play *Hobson's Choice* by Harold Brighouse (1915), filmed in 1954 by David Lean, a comedic adaptation?

Story Credit:
Geoffrey of Monmouth, *The History of the Kings of Britain* (1136?)
True Chronical History of King Leir, a play, anonymously written, before 1594.

For the Gloucester/Edmund/Edgar subplot:
John Higgins, *A Mirror for Magistrates*, (1574)
Raphael Holinshed, *Chronicles of England, Scotland, and Ireland* (1577)
William Warner, *Albion's England* (1586)
Edmund Spenser, *The Fairie Queen* (1590)
Sir Phillip Sidney's *Arcadia* (1593) and (for the names of Poor Tom's demons) Samuel Harsnett's *Declaration of Egregious Popish Imposters* (1593)

www.ingramcontent.com/pod-product-compliance
Lightning Source LLC
Chambersburg PA
CBHW061944070426
42450CB00007BA/1043